Essential English

# 基礎英語

Written by:

Christopher Warnasch

Translated by:

Mamori Sugita Hughes

Edited by:

Laura Riggio

**LIVING LANGUAGE®**

Published in the United States by Living Language, an imprint of Random House, Inc.

www.livinglanguage.com

Editor: Laura Riggio
Production Editor: Ciara Robinson
Production Manager: Tom Marshall
Interior Design: Sophie Chin
Illustrations: Sophie Chin

First Edition

ISBN: 978-0-307-97246-0

This book is available at special discounts for bulk purchases for sales promotions or premiums. Special editions, including personalized covers, excerpts of existing books, and corporate imprints, can be created in large quantities for special needs. For more information, write to Special Markets/ Premium Sales, 1745 Broadway, MD 3-1, New York, New York 10019 or e-mail specialmarkets@ randomhouse.com.

PRINTED IN THE UNITED STATES OF AMERICA
10 9 8 7 6 5 4 3 2 1

## Acknowledgments

Thanks to the Living Language team: Amanda D'Acierno, Christopher Warnasch, Suzanne McQuade, Laura Riggio, Erin Quirk, Amanda Munoz, Fabrizio LaRocca, Siobhan O'Hare, Sophie Chin, Pat Stango, Sue Daulton, Alison Skrabek, Ciara Robinson, and Tom Marshall.

COURSE

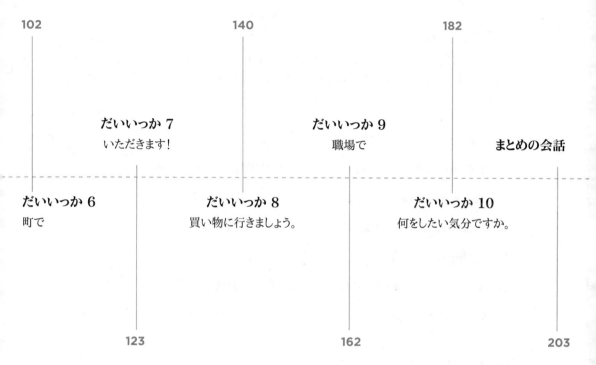
OUTLINE

# イントロダクション

*Living Language Essential English* へようこそ! 入念に練られた豊富な用例を通して、語彙や文法を分かりやすく学んでいくことができます。

## LESSONS

*Essential English* は全 10 課から構成されており、様々なシチュエーションで役立つ語彙や基本文法を紹介していきます。それぞれの課には以下の項目が盛り込まれています。

- **Welcome:** 本課で学習する内容の紹介

- **Vocabulary Builder 1 and 2:** 本課のトピックに関連した重要語句

- **Vocabulary Practice 1 and 2:** 新出語句を中心とした演習

- **Grammar Builder 1 and 2:** 重要文法事項の説明と用例

- **Work Out 1 and 2:** 新出文法や語句を中心とした演習

- **Bring It All Together:** 新しく学んだ文法を使った会話や文章

- **Drive It Home:** 何も考えることなく文法がすらすらと出てくるようになるための重要な演習

- **Parting Words:** 本課で学習したことのまとめ

- **Take It Further:** もう少し深くつっこんで学びたい人のための情報源

## WORD RECALL

各課の終わりには **Word Recall** があり、前課で学習した重要単語を忘れないようにするために設けられています。

## QUIZZES

Lesson 5 の後に **Quiz 1**、Lesson 10 の後に **Quiz 2** が設けられています。自己採点してもう一度復習するべき点を確認してください。

## REVIEW DIALOGUES

本書の終わりには日常英会話の学習に役立つ5つの会話が用意されています。それ
ぞれの会話には内容の理解度を確認するためのテストがついています。

## PROGRESS BAR

**Progress Bar** で本書における学習の進み具合を確認することができます。

## AUDIO

▶のマークは音声が CD で聞けることを表しています。CD のトラックナンバーも一緒
に記載されています。▶ のマークが見当たらない場合は、そのセクションのオーディ
オはないということです。

## GRAMMAR SUMMARY

巻末には **Grammar Summary** があり、*Essential English* で網羅されている全ての文
法事項を確認することができます。

## FREE ONLINE TOOLS

こちらのページでは、学習に役立つ様々なツールを無料で利用することができま
す。www.livinglanguage.com/languagelab 画像と音声付きのバーチャル単語カ
ードや学習内容の理解度を確認できるゲームが用意されています。

Hello! How Are You?    Big or Small? Short or Tall?    Everyday Life

This Is My Family    Welcome to My Home

# だいいっか 1: こんにちは!お元気ですか。

**Lesson 1: Hello! How Are You?**

**Hello!** (こんにちは!) 本課では、基本表現と今日からすぐに使える単語やフレーズを学習します。レッスン内容は以下の通りです。

☐ **hello** や **my name is ...** といった表現

☐ **how are you?** と尋ね、**I'm fine** などと答える

☐ **from** を使って出身を言う

☐ **I am, you are, she is** といった **be** 動詞の使い方

☐ 学習した表現を会話で実際に使ってみる

　　▶ のマーク は付属のCDで音声が聞けることを示します。それでは始めましょう!

## Vocabulary Builder 1

▶ 1A Vocabulary Builder 1 (CD 1, Track 2)

| Hi! | こんにちは！/どうも！ |
|---|---|
| Hello! | こんにちは！ |
| Good morning! | おはようございます！ |
| How are you? | お元気ですか。 |
| I'm fine, thanks! | 元気です。ありがとうございます！ |
| What's your name? | お名前は何ですか。 |
| My name is John. | 私の名前はジョンです。 |
| Where are you from? | ご出身はどちらですか。 |
| I'm from Boston. | 出身はボストンです。 |
| What do you do, John? | ジョンさん、ご職業は何ですか。 |
| I'm a student at the university. | 私は大学の学生です。 |
| Nice to meet you! | お会いできて嬉しいです！ / どうぞよろしく！ |
| Good-bye! | さようなら！ |

## ✎ Vocabulary Practice 1

▶ 1B Vocabulary Practice 1 (CD 1, Track 3)

ボキャブラリーの練習です。音声を聞いて空欄を埋めてください。

1. _____!

2. _____!

3. Good _____!

4. How _____ you?

5. I'm _____, thanks.

Hello! How Are You?          Big or Small? Short or Tall?          Everyday Life

This Is My Family                    Welcome to My Home

6. _____ your name?

7. _____ name is John.

8. _____ are you _____?

9. _____ from Boston.

10. I'm a _____ at the _____.

11. Nice _____ meet you.

12. _____.

**答え**

1. Hi! 2. Hello! 3. morning; 4. are; 5. fine; 6. What's; 7. My; 8. Where, from; 9. I'm; 10. student, university; 11. to; 12. Good-bye.

# Grammar Builder 1

▶ 1C Grammar Builder 1 (CD 1, Track 4)

## HELLO! HOW ARE YOU?

(午前 9:30)

| Good morning, John! | ジョンさん、おはようございます！ |
|---|---|
| Hi, Mary. How are you? | こんにちはメアリーさん。お元気ですか。 |
| I'm fine, thanks. And you? | 元気です。ありがとうございます。ジョンさんは？ |
| I'm good. | 元気です。 |

(午後 2:00)

| Hello, Professor Ramirez. | ラミレズ先生、こんにちは。 |
|---|---|
| Good afternoon, Mary. How are you doing? | メアリーさん、こんにちは。元気ですか。 |

| Very well, thank you. | とても元気です。ありがとうございます。 |

(午後 7:00)

| Good evening, Mr. Johnson. | ジョンソンさん、こんばんは。 |
| Good evening, Mrs. Chang. It's so nice to see you. | チャンさん、こんばんは。お会いできてとても嬉しいです。 |

(午後 11:00)

| Good-bye, John. | ジョンさん、さようなら。 |
| Good night, Mary. | メアリーさん、おやすみなさい。 |

## Take it Further

▶ 1D Take It Further (CD 1, Track 5)

**how are you?** (お元気ですか。)と聞かれたら

| | **I'm great!** や **I'm fantastic!** や **I'm really good!** (とても元気です!)、または **I'm fine.** や **I'm good.** (元気です。)<br>または |
| | **I'm okay.** や **So-so.** (まあまあです。)<br>または |
| | **Not well.** や **Not good.** (元気ではありません。)<br>と言ってみましょう。 |

Hello! How Are You?　　　　Big or Small? Short or Tall?　　　　Everyday Life

This Is My Family　　　　　　Welcome to My Home

how are you? の代わりに how's it going?（元気?/調子はどう?）と言うと、フレンドリーでカジュアルになります。フレンドリーでカジュアルな答え方としては

| | |
|---|---|
|  | **Great!** や**Fantastic!** や **Really well!**（とても元気だよ!）または **Fine.** や **Well.**（元気だよ。）<br>または |
|  | **Okay.** や **So-so.**（まあまあだよ。）<br>または |
|  | **Not well.**（元気じゃないよ。）<br>といったものがあります。 |

# Vocabulary Builder 2

▶ 1E Vocabulary Builder 2 (CD 1, Track 6)

| | |
|---|---|
| **This is John.** | こちらはジョンさんです。 |
| **John is from Boston, in the United States.** | 彼はアメリカのボストンの出身です。 |
| **He is American.** | ジョンさんはアメリカ人です。 |
| **This is Hiroko.** | こちらは広子さんです。 |
| **Hiroko is from Tokyo, in Japan.** | 広子さんは日本の東京の出身です。 |
| **She is Japanese.** | 彼女は日本人です。 |
| **This is Diego.** | こちらはディエゴさんです。 |
| **Diego is from Guadalajara, in Mexico.** | ディエゴさんはメキシコのグアダラハラの出身です。 |
| **He is Mexican.** | ディエゴさんはメキシコ人です。 |

| This is Li. | こちらはリーさんです。 |
|---|---|
| Li is from Beijing, in China. | リーさんは中国の北京の出身です。 |
| Li is Chinese. | リーさんは中国人です。 |
| This is Ahmed. | こちらはアーメッドさんです。 |
| Ahmed is from Cairo, in Egypt. | アーメッドさんはエジプトのカイロの出身です。 |
| He is Egyptian. | 彼さんはエジプト人です。 |
| This is Martine. | こちらはマーティンさんです。 |
| Martine is from Paris, in France. | マーティンさんはフランスのパリの出身です。 |
| Martine is French. | マーティンさんはフランス人です。 |

# ✎ Vocabulary Practice 2

空欄に適切な国籍を埋めてください。

1. John is from Boston, so he's _____.

2. Hiroko is from Tokyo, so she's _____.

3. Li is from Beijing, so he's _____.

4. Diego is from Guadalajara, so he's _____.

5. Ahmed is from Cairo, so he's _____.

6. Martine is from Paris, so she's _____.

**答え**
1. American; 2. Japanese; 3. Chinese; 4. Mexican; 5. Egyptian; 6. French

今度は国名を空欄に埋めてください。

1. Beijing is in _____.

Hello! How Are You?    Big or Small? Short or Tall?    Everyday Life

This Is My Family    Welcome to My Home

2. Cairo is in _____.

3. Boston is in _____.

4. Paris is in _____.

5. Guadalajara is in _____.

6. Tokyo is in _____.

### 答え
1. China; 2. Egypt; 3. the United States; 4. France; 5. Mexico; 6. Japan

# Grammar Builder 2

▶ 1F Grammar Builder 2 (CD 1, Track 7)

### 動詞 TO BE

| | |
|---|---|
| I am (I'm)<br>私は～です | we are (we're)<br>私達は～です |
| you are (you're)<br>あなたは～です | you are (you're)<br>あなた達は～です |
| he is, she is, it is (he's, she's, it's)<br>彼は～です、彼女は～です、それは～です | they are (they're)<br>彼ら/彼女ら/それらは～です |

例文を見てみましょう。

| | |
|---|---|
| I'm John. I'm a student. I'm from Boston. | 私はジョンです。学生です。ボストンの出身です。 |
| You're Hiroko, and you're from Japan. | あなたは広子さんで、日本の出身です。 |
| This is Diego. He's from Mexico. | こちらはディエゴさんです。彼はメキシコの出身です。 |

| We're Martine and François. We're French. | 私達はマーティンとフランソワです。私達はフランス人です。 |
| Ahmed and Layla, you're from Cairo. | アーメッドさん、ライラさん、あなた達はカイロの出身です。 |
| Li and Ming are from Beijing. They're Chinese. | リーさんとミンさんは北京の出身です。彼らは中国人です。 |

# ✎ Work Out 1

▶ 1G Work Out 1 (CD 1, Track 8)

音声を聞いて空欄を埋めてください。

1. Diego _____ from Guadalajara.

2. Maria _____ from Guadalajara, too.

3. Martine and François _____ French.

4. John _____ a student.

5. Where _____ you from?

6. I _____ from New York.

7. She _____ from Delhi.

8. How _____ they doing?

9. Ahmed _____ in Cairo.

10. Ahmed and Layla _____ in Cairo.

**答え**
1. is; 2. is; 3. are; 4. is; 5. are; 6. am; 7. is; 8. are; 9. is; 10. are

Hello! How Are You?   Big or Small? Short or Tall?   Everyday Life

This Is My Family   Welcome to My Home

## 🎧 Bring It All Together

▶ 1H Bring It All Together (CD 1, Track 9)

学習した内容を盛り込んだ会話を聞いてみましょう。ジョンさんはボストンの大学の学生です。授業が始まる前日にパーティーに行きました。ジョンさんはメアリーさんに自己紹介します。さて、どうなるか聞いてみましょう。

| | |
|---|---|
| **John:** | **Hi.** |
| ジョン： | どうも。 |
| **Mary:** | **Oh, hi there.** |
| メアリー： | ああ、どうも。 |
| **John:** | **I'm John. What's your name?** |
| ジョン： | 僕はジョン。名前は？ |
| **Mary:** | **Hi, John. I'm Mary. Nice to meet you.** |
| メアリー： | こんにちは、ジョン。私はメアリーよ。どうぞよろしく。 |
| **John:** | **Nice to meet you, too. So, Mary, how's it going?** |
| ジョン： | こちらこそよろしく。メアリー、調子はどう？ |
| **Mary:** | **Fine, thanks.** |
| メアリー： | いいわよ。ありがとう。 |
| **Mary:** | **Yeah, it's a good party.** |
| メアリー： | いいパーティーね。 |
| **John:** | **Are you a student here at the university?** |
| ジョン： | メアリーはここの大学の学生？ |
| **Mary:** | **No, I'm not a student.** |
| メアリー： | いいえ、学生じゃないわ。 |
| **John:** | **What do you do?** |
| ジョン： | じゃぁ、何をしてるの？ |
| **Mary:** | **I'm a professor.** |
| メアリー： | 私は教授よ。 |
| **John:** | **Oh ... A professor of what?** |
| ジョン： | あぁ・・・何の教授ですか。 |
| **Mary:** | **American literature.** |

| | |
|---|---|
| メアリー: | アメリカ文学よ。 |
| John: | Hmm … I have a class tomorrow. American literature of the … |
| ジョン: | えっと・・・僕は明日授業があるんです。20世紀アメリカ・・・ |
| Mary: | … Twentieth Century? |
| メアリー: | 文学? |
| John: | Yes, that's the one. |
| ジョン: | はい、それです。 |
| Mary: | Well, John, I'll see you in class tomorrow! |
| メアリー: | それじゃあジョン、明日授業で会いましょうね! |
| John: | Oh, right. Well, um, good night … |
| ジョン: | はい、そうですね。えっと、あの、おやすみなさい・・・ |
| Mary: | … Professor Wheaton. Good night, John. Very nice to meet you! |
| メアリー: | ウィートン(先生)です。お休みなさい、ジョン。お会いできてよかったわ! |

# ✎ Work Out 2

下のリストから適切な単語を選んで空欄を埋めてください。

student, meet, are, I'm, your, university, name, nice, thanks

Bill: **Hi. My (1)** _____ **is Bill. What's (2)** _____ **name?**
Peter: **I'm Peter.**
Bill: **How (3)** _____ **you, Peter?**
Peter: **I'm fine, (4)**_____. **And you?**
Bill: **I'm good.**
Peter: **Are you a (5)**_____ **at the**
**(6)**_____ **?**
Bill: **Yes. And you?**
Peter: **(7)**_____ **a student here, too.**
Bill: **(8)**_____ **to meet you, Peter.**
Peter: **Nice to (9)**_____ **you, too.**

**答え**
1. name; 2. your; 3. are; 4. thanks; 5. student; 6. university; 7. I'm; 8. Nice; 9. Meet

だいいっか 1: Hello! How Are You?     **17**

Hello! How Are You?        Big or Small? Short or Tall?        Everyday Life

This Is My Family                    Welcome to My Home

適切な単語を選んでください。

1. John _____ from Boston.

   a. am

   b. are

   c. is

   d. be

2. Marie is from Paris. _____ is French.

   a. He

   b. She

   c. I

   d. You

3. Diego and Maria _____ from Mexico.

   a. he

   b. is

   c. they

   d. are

4. _____ are Mexican.

   a. I

   b. They

   c. He

   d. She

5. I _____ a student at the university.

   a. am

Around Town    Let's Go Shopping   What Do You Feel Like Doing?

Let's Eat!      At Work

b. is

c. be

d. are

6. It's _____ to meet you, Mrs. Chang.

 a. here

 b. fine

 c. nice

 d. so-so

**答え**
1. c; 2. b; 3. d; 4. b; 5. a; 6. c

## ✎ Drive It Home

もう少し練習してみましょう。下の例にならってください。

例: John, the United States.
答え: John is from the United States. He is American.

1. Hiroko, Japan

_____

2. Ahmed, Egypt

_____

3. Diego, Mexico

_____

4. Martine, France

_____

Hello! How Are You?      Big or Small? Short or Tall?      Everyday Life

This Is My Family      Welcome to My Home

5. Li, China

---

**答え**

1. Hiroko is from Japan. She is Japanese. 2. Ahmed is from Egypt. He is Egyptian. 3. Diego is from Mexico. He is Mexican. 4. Martine is from France. She is French. 5. Li is from China. He is Chinese.

## Parting Words

**Well done!**（よくできました！）これで最初の英語のレッスンは終了です。本課で学習した内容を確認してみましょう。

☐ **hello** と **my name is …** といった表現　（まだ自信がない場合は p. 9 に戻って復習しましょう。）

☐ **how are you?** と尋ね、**I'm fine** などと答える　（まだ自信がない場合は p. 10 に戻って復習しましょう。）

☐ **from** を使って出身を言う　（まだ自信がない場合は p. 12 に戻って復習しましょう。）

☐ **I am, you are, she is,** といった **be** 動詞の使い方　（まだ自信がない場合は p. 14 に戻って復習しましょう。）

☐ 学習した表現を会話で実際に使ってみる　（まだ自信がない場合は p. 16 に戻って復習しましょう。）

---

## Take it Further

▶ 1G Take It Further (CD 1, Track 10)

色々な countries（国）, nationalities（国籍），そして languages（言語）を見てみましょう。

| | |
|---|---|
| **People from Mexico are Mexican, and they speak Spanish.** | メキシコ出身の人はメキシコ人で、彼らはスペイン語を話します。 |
| **People from China are Chinese, and they speak Mandarin and other languages.** | 中国出身の人は中国人で、彼らは標準中国語やその他の言語を話します。 |

| People from India are Indian, and they speak Hindi and other languages. | インド出身の人はインド人で、彼らはヒンズー語やその他の言語を話します。 |
| People from Canada are Canadian, and they speak English and French. | カナダ出身の人はカナダ人で、彼らは英語とフランス語を話します。 |
| People from Japan are Japanese, and they speak Japanese. | 日本出身の人は日本人で、彼らは日本語を話します。 |
| People from Egypt are Egyptian, and they speak Arabic. | エジプト出身の人はエジプト人で、彼らはアラビア語を話します。 |
| People from Russia are Russian, and they speak Russian. | ロシア出身の人はロシア人で、彼らはロシア語を話します。 |
| People from the United Kingdom are British, and they speak English. | イギリス出身の人はイギリス人で、彼らは英語を話します。 |
| People from France are French, and they speak French. | フランス出身の人はフランス人で、彼らはフランス語を話します。 |
| People from Brazil are Brazilian, and they speak Portuguese. | ブラジル出身の人はブラジル人で、彼らはポルトガル語を話します。 |
| People from Korea are Korean, and they speak Korean. | 韓国出身の人は韓国人で、彼らは韓国語を話します。 |

What country are you from?
あなたはどちらの国の出身ですか？

What language do you speak?
あなたは何語を話しますか？

www.livinglanuage.com/languagelab のページをチェックするのを忘れずに。バーチャル単語帳やゲームやクイズで、学習したことを復習してみましょう！

# Word Recall

第1課で出てきた単語を覚えたか確認しましょう。空欄を埋めてください。

1. _____ morning!

2. _____ are you?

3. _____ fine, thanks!

4. _____ your name?

5. Where are you _____?

6. I'm a _____ at the university.

7. _____ is Hiroko.

8. Hiroko _____ from Tokyo, in Japan.

9. _____ is Japanese.

10. This _____ Diego.

11. Diego is from Guadalajara, _____ Mexico.

12. _____ is Mexican.

答え
1. Good; 2. How; 3. I'm; 4. What's; 5. from; 6. student; 7. This; 8. is; 9. She; 10. is; 11. in; 12. He

Essential English

# だいいっか 2: これは私の家族です。

## Lesson 2: This Is My Family

Hello again!（またお会いしましたね!）本課では、人々と家族について話します。レッスン内容は以下の通りです。

□ people や family に関する基礎的な語彙

□ 動詞 to have

□ family に関連した更なる語彙

□ my, your, his, her, John's といった所有を表す言葉

□ 家族写真についての会話の中で学習した項目を総合的に使う
それでは始めましょう。準備はいいですか?

# Vocabulary Builder 1

2A Vocabulary Builder 1 (CD 1, Track 11)

| | |
|---|---|
| This is Paul Archer. | こちらはポール・アーチャーさんです。 |
| He is a man. | 彼は男性です。 |
| This is Laura Archer. | こちらはローラ・アーチャーさんです。 |
| She is a woman. | 彼女は女性です。 |
| This is Jenny Archer. | こちらはジェニー・アーチャーさんです。 |
| She is a girl. | 彼女は女の子です。 |
| This is Billy Archer. | こちらはビリー・アーチャーさんです。 |
| He is a boy. | 彼は男の子です。 |
| This is the Archer family. | こちらはアーチャー一家です。 |
| Paul Archer is the father. | ポール・アーチャーさんはお父さんです。 |
| Laura Archer is the mother. | ローラ・アーチャーさんはお母さんです。 |
| Jenny Archer is the daughter. | ジェニー・アーチャーさんは娘さんです。 |
| And Billy Archer is the son. | そして、ビリー・アーチャーさんは息子さんです。 |

# Vocabulary Practice 1

空欄を埋めてください。

1. Laura Archer is a ________________.
2. In the Archer family, she is the ________________.
3. Billy is a _________.
4. In the Archer family, he is the _________.
5. Jenny is a __________.

Around Town · · · · · · · · · · Let's Go Shopping · · · · · · What Do You Feel Like Doing?

Let's Eat! · · · · · · · · · · · · · · · At Work

6. **In the Archer family, she is the** _____.

7. **Paul Archer is a** _____.

8. **In the Archer family, he is the** _____.

**答え**
1. woman; 2. mother; 3. boy; 4. son; 5. girl; 6. daughter; 7. man; 8. father

# Grammar Builder 1
▶ 2B Grammar Builder 1 (CD 1, Track 12)

**動詞 TO HAVE**

第1課では、とても重要な動詞 **to be** を学習しました。今回はもう一つの重要な動詞 である **to have** を見てみましょう。

| I have<br>私は〜がいます/〜があります/〜を持っています | we have<br>私達は〜がいます/〜があります/〜を持っています |
|---|---|
| you have<br>あなたは〜がいます/〜があります/〜を持っています | you have<br>あなた達は〜がいます/〜があります/〜を持っています |
| he has, she has, it has<br>彼は〜がいます/〜があります/〜を持っています、<br>彼女は〜がいます/〜があります/〜を持っています、<br>それは〜がいます/〜があります/〜を持っています | they have<br>彼ら/彼女ら/それらは<br>〜がいます/〜があります/〜を持っています |

例文を見てみましょう。

| Paul Archer has a wife, Laura Archer. | ポール・アーチャーさんには奥さんのローラ・アーチャーさんがいます。 |
|---|---|

Hello! How Are You?    Big or Small? Short or Tall?    Everyday Life

This Is My Family    Welcome to My Home

| Laura Archer has a husband, Paul Archer. | ローラ・アーチャーさんにはご主人のポール・アーチャーさんがいます。 |
| Paul and Laura Archer have children. | ポール・アーチャーさんとローラ・アーチャーさんはお子さんがいます。 |
| They have a daughter, Jenny. | 彼らには娘さんのジェニーさんがいます。 |
| They also have a son, Billy. | 彼らには息子さんのビリーさんもいます。 |
| Jenny has a brother, Billy. | ジェニーさんには弟さん（お兄さん）のビリーさんがいます。 |
| And Billy has a sister, Jenny. | そしてビリーさんにはお姉さん（妹さん）のジェニーさんがいます。 |
| They have parents, a mother and a father. | 彼らには両親、すなわちお母さんとお父さんがいます。 |

## Take it Further

▶ 2C Take It Further (CD 1, Track 13)

mother, father, daughter, そして son という単語はもう学習しましたね。でも parents にも parents がいますよ！

| Paul Archer's father is Tom Archer. | ポール・アーチャーさんのお父さんはトム・アーチャーさんです。 |
| Tom Archer is Billy and Jenny's grandfather. | トム・アーチャーさんはビリーさんとジェニーさんのおじいさんです。 |
| Paul Archer's mother is Betty Archer. | ポール・アーチャーさんのお母さんはベティー・アーチャーさんです。 |
| Betty Archer is Billy and Jenny's grandmother. | ベティー・アーチャーさんはビリーさんとジェニーさんのおばあさんです。 |

| | |
|---|---|
| Tom and Betty Archer are Billy and Jenny's grandparents. | トム・アーチャーさんとベティー・アーチャーさんはビリーさんとジェニーさんの祖父母です。 |
| Jenny is Tom and Betty's granddaughter. | ジェニーさんは、トムさんとベティーさんの孫娘です。 |
| Billy is Tom and Betty's grandson. | ビリーさんはトムさんとベティーさんの孫息子です。 |
| Jenny and Billy are Tom and Betty's grandchildren. | ジェニーさんとビリーさんは、トムさんとベティーさんのお孫さんです。 |

## Vocabulary Builder 2

▶ 2D Vocabulary Builder 2 (CD 1, Track 14)

| | |
|---|---|
| Laura Archer's brother is Brian Smith. | ローラ・アーチャーさんのお兄さん（弟さん）はブライアン・スミスさんです。 |
| Brian has a wife, Sarah Smith. | ブライアンさんには奥さんのサラ・スミスさんがいます。 |
| Brian and Sarah have a son, Max. | ブライアンさんとサラさんには息子さんのマックスさんがいます。 |
| Brian Smith is Billy and Jenny's uncle. | ブライアン・スミスさんはビリーさんとジェニーさんの伯父さん（叔父さん）です。 |
| Sarah Smith is Billy and Jenny's aunt. | サラ・スミスさんはビリーさんとジェニーさんの伯母さん（叔母さん）です。 |
| Max is Billy and Jenny's cousin. | マックスさんはビリーさんとジェニーさんのいとこです。 |
| Billy is Brian and Sarah's nephew. | ビリーさんはブライアンさんとサラさんの甥です。 |
| Jenny is Brian and Sarah's niece. | ジェニーさんはブライアンさんとサラさんの姪です。 |

Hello! How Are You?　　　Big or Small? Short or Tall?　　　Everyday Life

This Is My Family　　　　　　Welcome to My Home

## ✎ Vocabulary Practice 2

▷ 2E Vocabulary Practice 2 (CD 1, Track 15)

ボキャブラリーの練習です。音声を聞いて空欄を埋めてください。

1. Laura Archer's _____ is Brian Smith.

2. Brian has a _____, Sarah Smith.

3. Brian and Sarah have a _____, Max.

4. Brian Smith is Billy and Jenny's _____.

5. Sarah Smith is Billy and Jenny's _____.

6. Max is Billy and Jenny's _____.

7. Billy is Brian and Sarah's _____.

8. Jenny is Brian and Sarah's _____.

**答え**
1. brother; 2. wife; 3. son; 4. uncle; 5. aunt; 6. cousin; 7. nephew; 8. niece

## Grammar Builder 2

▷ 2F Grammar Builder 2 (CD 1, Track 16)

### MY, YOUR, HIS ...

Grammar Builder 1で、動詞 to have を学習しました。今度は所有を表す他の表現を見てみましょう。

| my<br>私の | our<br>私達の |
|---|---|
| your<br>あなたの | your<br>あなた達の |

| his, her, its<br>彼の、彼女の、その | their<br>彼らの/彼女らの/それらの |
|---|---|

例文を見てみましょう。

| I have a brother. My brother is Billy. | 私は弟（兄）がいます。私の弟（兄）はビリーです。 |
|---|---|
| You have a sister. Your sister is Jenny. | あなたはお姉さん（妹さん）がいます。あなたのお姉さん（妹さん）はジェニーさんです。 |
| She has a cousin. Her cousin is Max. | 彼女はいとこがいます。彼女のいとこはマックスさんです。 |
| He has a cousin, too. His cousin is Max. | 彼もいとこがいます。彼のいとこはマックスさんです。 |
| We have a son. Our son is Billy. | 私達は息子がいます。私達の息子はビリーです。 |
| They have a daughter. Their daughter is Jenny. | 彼らは娘さんがいます。彼らの娘さんはジェニーさんです。 |

それから 's も以下のような文で出てきましたね。

**Laura Archer's brother is Brian Smith. = Her brother is Brian Smith.**
ローラ・アーチャーさんのお兄さん（弟さん）はブライアン・スミスさんです。= 彼女のお兄さん（弟さん）はブライアン・スミスさんです。

**Max is Billy and Jenny's cousin. = Max is their cousin.**
マックスさんはビリーさんとジェニーさんのいとこです。= マックスさんは彼らのいとこです。

Hello! How Are You?        Big or Small? Short or Tall?        Everyday Life

This Is My Family                          Welcome to My Home

## ✎ Work Out 1

▶ 1I Work Out 1 (CD 1, Track 17)

音声を聞いて空欄を埋めてください。

1. This is my cousin. _____ name is Jack.

2. Jack _____ a sister. _____ name is Anne.

3. Jack and _____ mother is a professor.

4. _____ father is a professor, too.

5. They _____ a cousin.

6. _____ cousin's name is Gary.

7. _____ name is Chris.

8. What's _____ name?

**答え**
1. His; 2. has, Her; 3. Anne's; 4. Their; 5. have; 6. Their; 7. My; 8. your

## 🗨 Bring It All Together

▶ 2G Bring It All Together (CD 1, Track 18)

ジェニーさんがグレッグさんに家族写真を見せています。聞いてみましょう。

| | |
|---|---|
| Greg: | Is this your family in the photo? |
| グレッグ： | この写真に写っているのはジェニーの家族？ |
| Jenny: | Yes. |
| ジェニー： | そうよ。 |
| Greg: | Who is this man? |
| グレッグ： | この男の人は誰？ |
| Jenny: | That's my father. He's a professor at the university. |
| ジェニー： | 父よ。大学の教授なの。 |

| | |
|---|---|
| **Greg:** | **And is that your mother?** |
| グレッグ： | それから、あれはお母さん？ |
| **Jenny:** | **Yes, that's my mother. She's a professor, too.** |
| ジェニー： | そう、母よ。母も教授なの。 |
| **Greg:** | **You have two brothers?** |
| グレッグ： | ジェニーは男兄弟が二人いるの？ |
| **Jenny:** | **No, I have one brother. This is my brother. His name is Joe.** |
| ジェニー： | いいえ、一人兄（弟）がいるわ。これが私の兄（弟）。名前はジョーよ。 |
| **Greg:** | **And who is the other boy?** |
| グレッグ： | それじゃぁこっちの男の子は誰？ |
| **Jenny:** | **He's my cousin, Michael.** |
| ジェニー： | 彼は私のいとこのマイケルよ。 |
| **Greg:** | **And these are your grandparents?** |
| グレッグ： | それからこれはジェニーのおじいさんとおばあさん？ |
| **Jenny:** | **Yes, this is my grandmother, and this is my grandfather.** |
| ジェニー： | うん、これが祖母で、これが祖父よ。 |
| **Greg:** | **Where are they from?** |
| グレッグ： | おばあさんとおじいさんの出身は？ |
| **Jenny:** | **They're from Chicago.** |
| ジェニー： | シカゴの出身よ。 |

# Take It Further

▶ 2H Take It Further (CD 1, Track 19)

会話の中で、グレッグは **you have two brothers?** と尋ねました。–s をつけると複数形になります。

| **one brother**<br>一人の兄（弟） | **two brothers**<br>二人の兄（弟） |
|---|---|
| **one sister**<br>一人の姉（妹） | **two sisters**<br>二人の姉（妹） |

Hello! How Are You?　　　Big or Small? Short or Tall?　　　Everyday Life

This Is My Family　　　　　　Welcome to My Home

| one boy 一人の男の子 | two boys 二人の男の子 |
| one girl 一人の女の子 | two girls 二人の女の子 |

不規則な複数形もあります。

| one man 一人の男性 | two men 二人の男性 |
| one woman 一人の女性 | two women 二人の女性 |
| one child 一人の子供 | two children 二人の子供 |

第3課では複数形について詳しく見ていきます。

## ✎ Work Out 2

have あるいは has を空欄に埋めてください。

1. I _____ two sisters.

2. My sister _____ a brother.

3. The boys _____ two cousins.

4. We _____ two grandmothers and two grandfathers.

5. My grandparents _____ six grandchildren.

6. Billy _____ a sister.

7. Mr. and Mrs. Archer _____ two children, a son and a daughter.

8. You _____ a brother and two sisters.

9. My mother _____ a husband.

10. And my father _____ a wife.

**答え**
1. have; 2. has; 3. have; 4. have; 5. have; 6. has; 7. have; 8. have; 9. has; 10; has

**my, your, his, her, our, their** のうちで適切なものを空欄に埋めてください。

1. You have a cousin. _____ cousin's name is Max.

2. I have two sisters. _____ names are Silvia and Maria.

3. We have a mother and a father. _____ names are Sue and Albert.

4. My uncle has a son. _____ name is Jeff.

5. My aunt has a daughter. _____ name is Teresa.

6. We have two children. _____ children's names are Billy and Jenny.

7. I have a sister. _____ sister's name is Jenny.

**答え**
1. Your; 2. Their; 3. Their; 4. His; 5. Her; 6. Our; 7. My

## ✎ Drive It Home

アーチャー一家について話してみましょう。ポールさん、ローラさん、そして彼らのお子さんのジェニーさんとビリーさんを覚えていますか? おじいさんのトムさんとおばあさんのベティーさん、それからローラさんのお兄さん(弟さん)のブライアン・スミスさん、ブライアンさんの奥さんのサラさん、そして息子さんのマックスさんも忘れずに!それでは適切な単語で以下の空欄を埋めてみてください。

I am Jenny Archer.

Hello! How Are You?　　　Big or Small? Short or Tall?　　　Everyday Life

This Is My Family　　　　　Welcome to My Home

1. Paul Archer is my _____.

2. Laura Archer is his _____, and my _____.

3. Billy is my _____, and I am his _____.

4. Max is our _____.

5. His _____ are Brian and Sarah Smith.

6. Brian Smith is my _____, and I am his _____.

7. Sarah Smith is my _____, and my brother Billy is her

   _____.

8. Tom Archer is my _____, and Betty Archer is my

   _____.

**答え**
1. father; 2. wife, mother; 3. brother, sister; 4. cousin; 5. parents; 6. uncle, niece; 7. aunt, nephew; 8. grandfather, grandmother

## Parting Words

**Great!**（よくできました！）家族に関するレッスンはこれで終了です。学習した内容を確認してみましょう。

☐ **people** や **family** に関する基礎的な語彙　（まだ自信がない場合は p. 24 に戻って復習しましょう。）

☐ 動詞 **to have** (まだ自信がない場合は p. 25 に戻って復習しましょう。)

☐ **family** に関連した更なる語彙　（まだ自信がない場合は p. 27 に戻って復習しましょう。）

☐ **my, your, his, her, John's** といった所有を表す言葉　（まだ自信がない場合は p. 28 に戻って復習しましょう。）

□ 家族写真についての会話の中で、学習した項目を総合的に使う　(まだ自信がない
　場合は p.30 に戻って復習しましょう。)

www.livinglanguage.com/languagelab のページをチェック
するのを忘れずに。バーチャル単語帳やゲームやクイズで、学習
したことを復習してみましょう!

# Word Recall

第2課で学んだ家族に関する語彙の復習をしましょう。

1. My brother's father is my _____.

2. My mother's daughter is my _____.

3. My mother's son is my _____.

4. My father's wife is my _____.

5. My mother's brother is my _____.

6. And my mother's sister is my _____.

7. My aunt and uncle's daughter is my _____.

8. I'm a girl; I am my father and mother's _____.

9. I'm a girl; I am my aunt and uncle's _____.

10. I'm a boy; I am my father and mother's _____.

11. I'm a boy; I am my aunt and uncle's _____.

12. My father's mother is my _____.

13. And my father's father is my _____.

14. My grandmother and grandfather are my _____.

**答え**
1. father; 2. sister; 3. brother; 4. mother; 5. uncle; 6. aunt; 7. cousin; 8. daughter; 9. niece; 10.
son; 11. nephew; 12. grandmother; 13. grandfather; 14. grandparents

**Essential English**

# だいいっか 3: 大きいですか、それとも小さいですか。背が低いですか、それとも背が高いですか。

## Lesson 3: Big or Small? Short or Tall?

**Welcome to Lesson 3!**（第3課へようこそ！）本課では big, small, short, そして tall といった形容詞を学習します。数も見ていきます。レッスン内容は以下の通りです。

☐ big, small, beautiful, ugly といった形容詞で人や物について説明する

☐ 動詞 be と have を使った yes/no で答えられる疑問文

☐ there is と there are

☐ 数と複数形

☐ ジョンさんの授業に関する会話の中で、学習した項目を総合的に使う
  それでは始めましょう！

Hello! How Are You?     Big or Small? Short or Tall?     Everyday Life

This Is My Family          Welcome to My Home

## Vocabulary Builder 1

▶ 3A Vocabulary Builder 1 (CD 1, Track 20)

| | |
|---|---|
| Canada is a big country. | カナダは大きい国です。 |
| Singapore is a small country. | シンガポールは小さい国です。 |
| Paris is a beautiful city. | パリは美しい都市です。 |
| Paris is not an ugly city. | パリは醜い都市ではありません。 |
| The Sahara is very hot. | サハラ砂漠はとても暑いです。 |
| Antarctica is very cold. | 南極はとても寒いです。 |
| The Amazon is a long river. | アマゾン川は長い川です。 |
| The Amazon is not short. | アマゾン川は短くありません。 |
| I am in New York; Philadelphia is near. | 私はニューヨークにいます。フィラデルフィアは近いです。 |
| I am in New York; Beijing is far. | 私はニューヨークにいます。北京は遠いです。 |
| Mr. Archer is a man; he is tall. | アーチャーさんは男性です。彼は背が高いです。 |
| Billy is a boy; he is short. | ビリーさんは男の子です。彼は背が低いです。 |
| Billy's grandfather is old. | ビリーさんのおじいさんは年をとっています。 |
| Billy is not old, he's young. | ビリーさんは年をとっていません。彼は若いです。 |
| My professor is excellent; she is very good. | 私の先生は優秀です。彼女はとてもいい（先生）です。 |
| Your professor is not good; he's bad! | あなたの先生は良くないです。彼は悪い（先生）です。 |
| 1+1 is easy. | 1+1 は簡単です。 |
| $2x(3y-4x)=2y/x$ is hard! | $2x(3y-4x)=2y/x$ は難しいです！ |

Around Town | Let's Go Shopping | What Do You Feel Like Doing?

Let's Eat! | At Work

## ✏️ Vocabulary Practice 1

ボキャブラリーの練習です。

1. China is not a small country; it's a _____ country.

2. The Amazon is not a short river; it's a _____ river.

3. My grandparents are not young; they are _____.

4. Antarctica is very _____.

5. Saudi Arabia is not cold; it's _____.

6. You're in Philadelphia, so New York is _____.

7. You're in Philadelphia, so Tokyo is _____.

8. My professor is not bad; he's very _____.

9. The woman is not _____; she's tall.

10. San Francisco is not an ugly city; it's a _____ city.

11. What's one plus one? That's an _____ question!

12. But the professor's question isn't easy; it's _____.

**答え**
1. big; 2. long; 3. old; 4. cold; 5. hot; 6. near; 7. far; 8. good; 9. short; 10. beautiful; 11. easy;
12. hard

---

## Take It Further

▶ 3B Take It Further (CD 1, Track 21)

**COLORS (色) はとても便利な形容詞です。**

| The sky at night is black. | 夜の空は黒いです。 |

だいいっか 3: Big or Small? Short or Tall?　　　**39**

Hello! How Are You?          Big or Small? Short or Tall?          Everyday Life

This Is My Family                    Welcome to My Home

| Snow is white. | 雪は白いです。 |
| Roses are red. | バラは赤いです。 |
| The ocean is blue. | 海は青いです。 |
| Plants are green. | 植物は緑です。 |
| Bananas are yellow. | バナナは黄色いです。 |
| Tea is brown. | 紅茶は茶色いです。 |
| Oranges are orange. | オレンジはオレンジ色です。 |
| Grapes are purple. | ブドウは紫です。 |
| Elephants are gray. | 象は灰色です。 |

もう少し例文を見てみましょう。

| The American flag is red, white, and blue. | アメリカの国旗は赤と白と青です。 |
| The Chinese flag is red and yellow. | 中国の国旗は赤と黄色です。 |
| The Indian flag is orange, green, white, and blue. | インドの国旗はオレンジと緑と白と青です。 |
| At night, the sky is black, but during the day, the sky is blue. | 夜は空は黒いですが、昼間は空は青いです。 |

# Grammar Builder 1

▶ 3C Grammar Builder 1 (CD 1, Track 22)

**YES ですか 、NO ですか?**

**Am** や **is** や **are** を使って疑問文を作りたい場合は、動詞を最初に持っていきます。

| I am ... <br> 私は・・・です。 | Am I ...? <br> 私は・・・ですか。 |

| | |
|---|---|
| **You are a professor.**<br>あなたは教授です。 | **Are you a professor?**<br>あなたは教授ですか。 |
| **He is Chinese.**<br>彼は中国人です。 | **Is he Chinese?**<br>彼は中国人ですか。 |
| **Martine is French.**<br>マーティンさんはフランス人です。 | **Is Martine French?**<br>マーティンさんはフランス人ですか。 |
| **We are at the university.**<br>私達は大学にいます。 | **Are we at the university?**<br>私達は大学にいますか。 |
| **The children are young.**<br>子供達は小さいです。 | **Are the children young?**<br>子供達は小さいですか。 |

be 動詞を使った質問に答えるには、yes と言うか no + not を使いましょう。

**Is New York a beautiful city?**
ニューヨークは美しい都市ですか。

**Yes, New York is a beautiful city.**
はい、ニューヨークは美しい都市です。
または
**No, New York is not a beautiful city.**
いいえ、ニューヨークは美しい都市ではありません。

**Is he a good professor?**
彼はいい先生ですか。

**Yes, he is a good professor.**
はい、彼はいい先生です。
または
**No, he is not a good professor.**
いいえ、彼はいい先生ではありません。

Hello! How Are You?　　　Big or Small? Short or Tall?　　　Everyday Life

This Is My Family　　　　Welcome to My Home

**Is Chicago far?**
シカゴは遠いですか。

**Yes, Chicago is far.**
はい、シカゴは遠いです。
または
**No, Chicago is not far.**
いいえ、シカゴは遠くありません。

**have** を疑問文するには **do ... have?** を使います。

| | |
|---|---|
| **I have ...**<br>私は・・・がいます。/があります。/を持っています。 | **Do I have ... ?**<br>私は・・・がいますか。/がありますか。/を持っていますか。 |
| **You have a sister.**<br>あなたは妹さんがいます。 | **Do you have a sister?**<br>あなたは妹さんがいますか。 |
| **They have children.**<br>彼らはお子さんがいます。 | **Do they have children?**<br>彼らはお子さんがいますか。 |

**has** を疑問文するには **does ... have?** を使います。

| | |
|---|---|
| **He has ...**<br>彼は・・・がいます。/があります。/を持っています。 | **Does he have ... ?**<br>彼は・・・がいますか。/がありますか。/を持っていますか。 |
| **She has ...**<br>彼女は・・・がいます。/があります。/を持っています。 | **Does she have ... ?**<br>彼女は・・・がいますか。/がありますか。/を持っていますか。 |
| **Jenny has a brother.**<br>ジェニーさんは弟さん（お兄さん）がいます。 | **Does Jenny have a brother?**<br>ジェニーさんは弟さん（お兄さん）がいますか。 |

| Billy has a sister. ビリーさんはお姉さん（妹さん）がいます。 | Does Billy have a sister? ビリーさんはお姉さん（妹さん）がいますか。 |
|---|---|

have を使った質問に答えるには、yes と言うか no + do not have を使いましょう。

**Do they have children?**
彼らはお子さんがいますか。

**Yes, they have children.**
はい、彼らはお子さんがいます。
または
**No, they do not have children.**
いいえ、彼らはお子さんはいません。

**Do we have a good professor?**
私達はいい先生がいますか。

**Yes, we have a good professor.**
はい、私達はいい先生がいます。
または
**No, we do not have a good professor.**
いいえ、私達はいい先生がいません。

has の疑問文に答えるには、yes と言うか no + does not have を使います。

**Does Bob have a wife?**
ボブさんは奥さんがいますか。

**Yes, he has a wife.**
はい、彼は奥さんがいます。
または

Hello! How Are You?　　　　Big or Small? Short or Tall?　　　　Everyday Life

This Is My Family　　　　Welcome to My Home

**No, he does not have a wife.**
いいえ、彼は奥さんはいません。

**Does Mrs. Archer have children?**
アーチャー夫人はお子さんがいますか。

**Yes, she has children.**
はい、彼女はお子さんがいます。
または
**No, she does not have children.**
いいえ、彼女はお子さんがいません。

## Take it Further

▶ 3D Take It Further (CD 1, Track 23)

第1課では **be** 動詞の標準形 (**I am, you are, he is, we are, they are**) と短縮形
(**I'm, you're, she's, we're, they're**) を学習しました。短縮形は **contractions** と言い
ます。**Not** の短縮形もあります。まずは **be** 動詞の短縮形から見ていきましょう。

| | |
|---|---|
| **Am I a professor?**<br>私は教授ですか。 | **No, I'm not a professor.**<br>いいえ、私は教授ではありません。 |
| **Are you a student?**<br>あなたは学生ですか。 | **No, you're not a student.**<br>**No, you aren't a student.**<br>いいえ、あなたは学生ではありません。 |
| **Is he a student?**<br>彼は学生ですか。 | **No he's not a student.**<br>**No he isn't a student.**<br>いいえ、彼は学生ではありません。 |
| **Are we in Boston?**<br>私達はボストンにいますか。 | **No, we're not in Boston.**<br>**No, we aren't in Boston.**<br>いいえ、私達はボストンにいません。 |

| Are they near?<br>彼ら/彼女ら/これらは近いですか。 | No, they're not near.<br>No, they aren't near.<br>いいえ、彼ら/彼女ら/これらは近くありません。 |

主語が I の時は短縮形は一つしかありません (I'm not)。けれども you, he, she, it, we, they の時は二種類の短縮形があります。代名詞 + be (I'm, you're, etc.) の短縮形と be + not (aren't, isn't, etc.) の短縮形です。

| 代名詞 + be | be + not |
|---|---|
| I'm not<br>私は〜ではありません | – |
| you're not<br>あなたは〜ではありません | you aren't<br>あなたは〜ではありません |
| he's not<br>彼は〜ではありません | he isn't<br>彼は〜ではありません |
| she's not<br>彼女は〜ではありません | she isn't<br>彼女は〜ではありません |
| it's not<br>それは〜ではありません | it isn't<br>それは〜ではありません |
| we're not<br>私達は〜ではありません | we aren't<br>私達は〜ではありません |
| they're not<br>彼ら/彼女ら/それらは〜ではありません | they aren't<br>彼ら/彼女ら/それらは〜ではありません |

動詞 have を使う時は do/does + not を短縮します。

| Do I have children?<br>私は子供がいますか。 | No, I don't have children.<br>いいえ、私は子供はいません。 |
| Do you have a son?<br>あなたは息子さんがいますか。 | No, you don't have a son.<br>いいえ、あなたは息子さんはいません。 |

Hello! How Are You?　　　Big or Small? Short or Tall?　　　Everyday Life

This Is My Family　　　　Welcome to My Home

| | |
|---|---|
| **Does he have a good professor?**<br>彼はいい先生がいますか。 | **No, he doesn't have a good professor.**<br>いいえ、彼はいい先生はいません。 |
| **Does she have a brother?**<br>彼女はお兄さん（弟さん）がいますか。 | **No, she doesn't have a brother.**<br>いいえ、彼女はお兄さん（弟さん）はいません。 |
| **Do we have cousins?**<br>私達はいとこがいますか。 | **No, we don't have cousins.**<br>いいえ、私達はいとこはいません。 |
| **Do they have a daughter?**<br>彼ら/彼女らは娘さんがいますか。 | **No, they don't have a daughter.**<br>いいえ、彼ら/彼女らは娘さんはいません。 |

## Vocabulary Builder 2

▶ 3E Vocabulary Builder 2 (CD 1, Track 24)

| | |
|---|---|
| **There is a good university in the city.** | この都市にはいい大学があります。 |
| **There are two good universities in the city.** | この都市には二つのいい大学があります。 |
| **There is an excellent professor at the university.** | この大学には優れた先生がいます。 |
| **There are excellent professors at the university.** | この大学には優れた先生方がいます。 |
| **There is a young girl in the family.** | 家族には小さい女の子がいます。 |
| **There are three young girls in the family.** | 家族には三人の小さい女の子がいます。 |
| **There are tall buildings in New York.** | ニューヨークには高いビルがあります。 |
| **There are long rivers in South America.** | 南アメリカには長い川があります。 |

| There is excellent wine from France. | フランスからの優れたワインがあります。 |
| There are beautiful cities in Europe. | ヨーロッパには美しい都市があります。 |

# ✎ Vocabulary Practice 2

▶ 3F Vocabulary Practice 2 (CD 1, Track 25)

音声を聞いて空欄を埋めてください。

1. _____ is a good university in the city.

2. There _____ two good universities in the city.

3. There _____ an excellent professor at the university.

4. _____ excellent professors at the university.

5. _____ a young girl in the family.

6. There are three young _____ in the family.

7. There are tall _____ in New York.

8. There are _____ rivers in South America.

9. _____ excellent wine from France.

10. There are beautiful _____ in Europe.

**答え**
1. There; 2. are; 3. is; 4. There are; 5. There is; 6. girls; 7. buildings; 8. long; 9. There is; 10. cities

Hello! How Are You?        Big or Small? Short or Tall?        Everyday Life

This Is My Family        Welcome to My Home

# Grammar Builder 2

▶ 3G Grammar Builder 2 (CD 1, Track 26)

### 数と複数形

英語で数を数えてみましょう。

| one, two, three | 1, 2, 3 |
|---|---|
| four, five, six | 4, 5, 6 |
| seven, eight | 7, 8 |
| nine, ten | 9, 10 |

11 から 19までのほとんどは語尾に –teen が付きます。

| eleven, twelve, thirteen | 11, 12, 13 |
|---|---|
| fourteen, fifteen, sixteen | 14, 15, 16 |
| seventeen, eighteen, nineteen | 17, 18, 19 |

20 から 90までの10で割れる数には –ty が付きます。

| twenty, thirty, forty | 20, 30, 40 |
|---|---|
| fifty, sixty, seventy | 50, 60, 70 |
| eighty, ninety, one hundred | 80, 90, 100 |

21, 32, 43といった数を言うには、二つの数を組み合わせます。

| twenty-one, twenty-two, twenty-three | 21, 22, 23 |
|---|---|
| thirty-four, thirty-five, thirty-six | 34, 35, 36 |
| forty-seven, fifty-eight, ninety-nine | 47, 58, 99 |

年齢を言う時は、**be** 動詞と数を組み合わせるか、**be + years old** という表現を使います。年齢を尋ねる時は **how old is/are … ?** を使います。

| | |
|---|---|
| **How old is Billy?**<br>ビリーさんは何歳ですか。 | **He's ten years old.**<br>彼は10歳です。 |
| **How old is Jenny?**<br>ジェニーさんは何歳ですか。 | **She's fourteen.**<br>彼女は14歳です。 |
| **How old is Billy and Jenny's grandmother?**<br>ビリーさんとジェニーさんのおばあさんは何歳ですか。 | **She's sixty-three.**<br>彼女は63歳です。 |
| **How old are Billy and Jenny?**<br>ビリーさんとジェニーさんは何歳ですか。 | **They are ten and fourteen years old.**<br>彼らは10歳と14歳です。 |

**one** の時は名詞の単数形を使います。**two** あるいはそれ以上の数の時は複数形を使います。ほとんどの名詞では **–s** を付ければ複数形になります。

| | |
|---|---|
| **one boy**<br>一人の男の子 | **two boys, three boys**<br>二人の男の子、三人の男の子 |
| **one student**<br>一人の学生 | **ten students, fifteen students**<br>十人の学生、十五人の学生 |
| **one professor**<br>一人の教授 | **five professors, twenty professors**<br>五人の教授、二十人の教授 |

**–y** で終わる名詞の場合、複数形の語尾は **–ies** になります。

| | |
|---|---|
| **one university**<br>一つの大学 | **two universities**<br>二つの大学 |
| **one country**<br>一つの国 | **three countries**<br>三つの国 |
| **one city**<br>一つの都市 | **four cities**<br>四つの都市 |

Hello! How Are You?　　　　Big or Small? Short or Tall?　　　　Everyday Life

This Is My Family　　　　　　Welcome to My Home

名詞の中には不規則な複数形を持つものもあります。

| | |
|---|---|
| one man<br>一人の男性 | two men<br>二人の男性 |
| one woman<br>一人の女性 | three women<br>三人の女性 |
| one child<br>一人の子供 | four children<br>四人の子供 |
| one person<br>一人の人 | ten people<br>十人の人 |

単数形には there is (there's) を、複数形には there are を使います。

| There is …<br>〜があります/います | There are …<br>〜があります/います |
|---|---|
| There is a good university in the city.<br>市にはいい大学があります。 | There are three good universities in the city.<br>市にはいい大学が三つあります。 |
| There is a very good student in the class.<br>クラスにとてもいい学生がいます。 | There are very good students in the class.<br>クラスにとてもいい学生(達)がいます。 |
| There is one boy in the family.<br>家族に男の子が一人います。 | There are three boys in the family.<br>家族に男の子が三人います。 |

# ✎ Work Out 1
▶ 3H Work Out 1 (CD 1, Track 27)

音声を聞いて、適切な単語で空欄を埋めてください。

1. Billy is a _____ boy. He is _____ years old.

2. He _____ a big family, he has a _____ family.

3. _____ four people in his family.

4. Billy's father's _____ is Paul.

5. _____ mother's name is Laura.

6. Billy _____ have a brother, but he _____ a sister.

7. His _____ name is Jenny.

8. Jenny is _____.

9. Billy and Jenny _____ a cousin.

10. His name is Max, and he is _____.

答え

1. young, ten; 2. doesn't have, small; 3. There are; 4. name; 5. His; 6. doesn't, has; 7. sister's; 8. fourteen; 9. have; 10. nine years old

## ⒸⒸ Bring It All Together

▶ 31 Bring It All Together (CD 1, Track 28)

第1課でジョンさんに会いましたね。ジョンさんは大学生です。20世紀アメリカ文学という授業をとっています。けれどもジョンさんはあまり優秀な学生ではないようです。ジョンさんと友人のダイアンさんとの会話を聞いてみましょう。

| | |
|---|---|
| **Diane:** | **Are you in Professor Wheaton's class?** |
| ダイアン： | ウィートン先生の授業はとってる？ |
| **John:** | **Yes, I am. It's American Literature of the Twentieth Century.** |
| ジョン： | うん、とってるよ。20世紀アメリカ文学の授業だよ。 |
| **Diane:** | **Is it a good class?** |
| ダイアン： | いい授業？ |
| **John:** | **Yes, it's very good, but it's hard!** |

だいいっか 3: Big or Small? Short or Tall?

Hello! How Are You?　　Big or Small? Short or Tall?　　Everyday Life

This Is My Family　　Welcome to My Home

| ジョン: | うん、とてもいいけど、難しいよ! |
|---|---|
| **Diane:** | **Is Professor Wheaton a good professor?** |
| ダイアン: | ウィートン先生はいい先生? |
| **John:** | **Yes, she's very smart, but her questions are hard! And the books are hard!** |
| ジョン: | うん、先生はとても頭がいいけれど、質問が難しいんだ!それから本も難しいんだよ! |
| **Diane:** | **How many students are there in the class?** |
| ダイアン: | クラスには何人学生がいるの? |
| **John:** | **There are twenty-three students in the class.** |
| ジョン: | クラスには23人学生がいるよ。 |
| **Diane:** | **Are there good students in the class?** |
| ダイアン: | クラスによくできる学生はいる? |
| **John:** | **Yes, there are three or four excellent students in the class.** |
| ジョン: | うん、3人か4人優秀な学生がクラスにいるよ。 |
| **Diane:** | **Are you an excellent student?** |
| ダイアン: | あなたは優秀な学生? |
| **John:** | **No, I'm not an excellent student.** |
| ジョン: | いや、僕は優秀な学生じゃないよ。 |
| **Diane:** | **Well, are you a good student?** |
| ダイアン: | それじゃあ、いい学生? |
| **John:** | **No, I'm not a good student. I'm an okay student.** |
| ジョン: | いや、いい学生じゃないよ。まあまあの学生だね。 |
| **Diane:** | **An okay student? Do you have homework tonight?** |
| ダイアン: | まあまあの学生?今夜宿題はある? |
| **John:** | **Yes, I have homework, but there's a party tonight, and …** |
| ジョン: | うん、宿題があるけど、今夜はパーティーがあって・・・ |
| **Diane:** | **John! You have homework tonight!** |
| ダイアン: | ジョン!あなたは今夜宿題があるのよ! |
| **John:** | **Yes, I do. But there's a party, and …** |
| ジョン: | うん、そうだけど、パーティーがあって・・・ |
| **Diane:** | **And you're not an excellent student!** |

Around Town   Let's Go Shopping   What Do You Feel Like Doing?

Let's Eat!       At Work

ダイアン:  あなたは優秀な学生じゃないのよ!

---

# Take It Further

▶ 3J Take it Further (CD 1, Track 29)

### 本課では YES/NO

で答えられる疑問文を学習しました。疑問文にはその他に疑問詞を使ったものがあります。第1課から第3課までに以下のような疑問文が出てきました。

**What?**
何?

**What's your name?**
あなたのお名前は何ですか?

**My name is John.**
私の名前はジョンです。

**Who?**
誰?

**Who is this man?**
この男性は誰ですか?

**He's my father.**
彼は父です。

**How?**
どう?/どのぐらい?

Hello! How Are You?  Big or Small? Short or Tall?  Everyday Life

This Is My Family  Welcome to My Home

**How are you?**
お元気ですか？

**I'm fine, thanks.**
元気です。ありがとうございます。

**How old is Billy?**
ビリーさんは何歳ですか？

**He's ten years old.**
ビリーさんは10歳です。

**How many?**
いくつ？

**How many students are there in the class?**
クラスに何人学生がいますか？

**There are twenty-three students in the class.**
クラスに23人学生がいます。

---

## ✎ Work Out 2

**there is** あるいは **there are** のうち、適切な方を空欄に埋めてください。

1. _____ very good wine from France.

2. _____ fifty states in the United States.

3. _____ tall buildings in New York.

4. _____ an excellent student in the class.

5. _____ twenty-three students in the class.

6. _____ two girls in the family.

7. _____ a very long river in Brazil.

8. _____ three children in the family.

**答え**

1. There is; 2. There are; 3. There are; 4. There is; 5. There are; 6. There are; 7. There is;
8. There are

正しい単語を選んでください。

1. You (have/has) three sisters.

2. (Do/Does) she have a brother?

3. Yes, she (have/has) a brother.

4. No, she (doesn't/don't) have a brother.

5. The man (have/has) a wife.

6. The man doesn't (have/has) a wife.

7. I (don't/doesn't) have a sister.

8. We don't (have/has) a big family.

**答え**

1. have; 2. Does; 3. has; 4. doesn't; 5. has; 6. have; 7. don't; 8. have

今度は疑問文を作ってみましょう。
例えば **She has a sister.** とあったら **Does she have a sister?** と疑問文に直してください
い。

Hello! How Are You?　　　Big or Small? Short or Tall?　　　Everyday Life

This Is My Family　　　　Welcome to My Home

1. He is tall.

   _____

2. The girls have a brother.

   _____

3. The family is big.

   _____

4. The professors are very good.

   _____

5. The students have an easy class.

   _____

6. The boy has a sister.

   _____

7. The river is long.

   _____

8. Canada and China are big countries.

   _____

**答え**

1. Is he tall? 2. Do the girls have a brother? 3. Is the family big? 4. Are the professors very good? 5. Do the students have an easy class? 6. Does the boy have a sister? 7. Is the river long? 8. Are Canada and China big countries?

Around Town | Let's Go Shopping | What Do You Feel Like Doing?

Let's Eat! | At Work

# ✎ Drive It Home

質問に対する答え方を復習してみましょう。まずは **be** 動詞からです。

例: **Is New York a beautiful city?**
**Yes, New York is a beautiful city.**
**No, New York is not a beautiful city.**

1. **Is it a big country?** (Yes, it … , No, it … )

   _____

2. **Is the professor good?** (Yes, she … , No, she … )

   _____

3. **Are the questions easy?** (Yes, they … , No, they … )

   _____

4. **Are the children very young?** (Yes, they … , No, they … )

   _____

   **答え**
   1. Yes, it's a big country./No, it isn't/it's not a big country. 2. Yes, she's good./No, she isn't/she's not good. 3. Yes, they're easy./No, they aren't/they're not easy. 4. Yes, they're young./No, they're not/they aren't young.

   それでは今度は動詞 **have** を使った質問に対する答え方を復習しましょう。

   例: **Do we have a good professor?**
   **Yes, we have a good professor.**
   **No, we don't have a good professor.**

1. **Does she have a brother?** (Yes, she … , No, she … )

   _____

Hello! How Are You?          Big or Small? Short or Tall?          Everyday Life

This Is My Family          Welcome to My Home

2. **Do they have children?** (Yes, they … , No, they … )

_____

3. **Does she have a husband?** (Yes, she … , No, she … )

_____

4. **Do the boys have a sister?** (Yes, they … , No, they … )

_____

**答え**
1. Yes, she has a brother./No, she doesn't have a brother. 2. Yes, they have children./No, they don't have children. 3. Yes, she has a husband./No, she doesn't have a husband. 4. Yes, they have a sister./No, they don't have a sister.

## Parting Words

**Terrific!**(素晴らしいです!)第3課はこれで終了です。学習した内容を確認してみましょう。

☐ big, small, beautiful, ugly といった形容詞で人や物について説明する (まだ自信がない場合は p.38 に戻って復習しましょう。)

☐ 動詞 be と have を使った yes/no で答えられる疑問文 (まだ自信がない場合は p.40 に戻って復習しましょう。)

☐ there is と there are (まだ自信がない場合は p.46 に戻って復習しましょう。)

☐ 数と複数形 (まだ自信がない場合は p.48 に戻って復習しましょう。)

☐ ジョンさんの授業に関する会話の中で、学習した項目を総合的に使う (まだ自信がない場合は p.51 に戻って復習しましょう。)

www.livinglanguage.com/languagelab のページをチェックするのを忘れずに。バーチャル単語帳やゲームやクイズで、学習したことを復習してみましょう!

# Word Recall

各文で使われている形容詞の反意語を書いてください。

1. Their class is not good, it's _____.

2. Monaco is not big, it's _____.

3. Paris is not ugly, it's _____.

4. Antarctica is not hot, it's _____.

5. Your city is not near, it's _____.

6. His sister is not short, she's _____.

7. Our question is not hard, it's _____.

8. The Mississippi River is not short, it's _____.

9. The Sahara is not cold, it's _____.

10. My family is not small, it's _____.

11. The boy is not old, he's _____.

12. His class is not easy, it's _____.

13. The city is not beautiful, it's _____.

14. My grandmother is not young, she's _____.

答え
1. bad; 2. small; 3. beautiful; 4. cold; 5. far; 6. tall; 7. easy; 8. long; 9. hot; 10. big; 11. young; 12. hard; 13. ugly; 14. old

Hello! How Are You?          Big or Small? Short or Tall?          Everyday Life

This Is My Family                    Welcome to My Home

# だいいっか 4: 私の家へようこそ!

**Lesson 4: Welcome to My Home**

**How are you?** (お元気ですか。)本課では家についての話題を扱います。レッスン内容は以下の通りです。

☐ 家やアパートの各部屋の名前

☐ the と a/an

☐ 家やアパートにある物の名前

☐ in, on, under といった前置詞

☐ 自分の家について説明をする

## Vocabulary Builder 1

4A Vocabulary Builder 1 (CD 1, Track 30)

| Do you live in an apartment or a house? | あなた達はアパートに住んでいますか、それとも一軒家に住んでいますか。 |
| We live in a house. | 私達は一軒家に住んでいます。 |
| The house has four bedrooms. | 家には寝室が4つあります。 |
| It also has a comfortable living room. | 心地良い居間もあります。 |
| It has a sunny kitchen. | 日当たりのいい台所があります。 |
| And it has a large dining room. | それから広いダイニングがあります。 |
| There are also two bathrooms in the house. | それから家にはバスルームが2つあります。 |
| And there's a quiet study with a desk, a new computer, and books. | そして、机と新しいパソコンと本がある静かな書斎があります。 |
| The house also has a garage. | 家には車庫もあります。 |
| And it has a big yard with grass, trees, and a garden. | そして、芝生と木と花壇のある大きな庭があります。 |
| Our family has a dog and a cat. | うちには犬と猫がいます。 |
| The dog is black, and the cat is white. | 犬は黒くて、猫は白いです。 |

## Vocabulary Practice 1

4B Vocabulary Practice 1 (CD 1, Track 31)

音声を聞いて空欄を埋めてください。

1. Do you live in an _____ or a _____ ?

2. We _____ in a house.

3. The house has four _____.

Hello! How Are You?     Big or Small? Short or Tall?     Everyday Life

This Is My Family     Welcome to My Home

4. It also has a comfortable _____ .

5. It has a sunny _____ .

6. And it has a large _____ .

7. There are _____ two _____ in the house.

8. And there's a quiet _____ with a _____ , a computer, and books.

9. The house also has a _____ .

10. And it has a big _____ with grass, trees, and a flower

    _____ .

11. Our family has _____ and _____ .

12. The dog is _____ , and the cat is _____ .

**答え**
1. apartment, house; 2. live; 3. bedrooms; 4. living room; 5. kitchen; 6. dining room; 7. also, bathrooms; 8. study, desk; 9. garage; 10. yard, garden; 11. a dog, a cat; 12. black; white

## Take It Further

▶ 4C Take It Further (CD 1, Track 32)

Vocabulary Builder 1 で出てきた新しい単語を見てみましょう。

**house** や **apartment** には **rooms**(部屋)があります。**bedroom, living room, kitchen, dining room, bathroom, study** という部屋が出てきました。それぞれの部屋は何をするために使われるでしょうか。

| People sleep in a bedroom. | 人々は寝室で眠ります。 |
|---|---|
| People watch television in a living room. | 人々は居間でテレビを見ます。 |

| People cook in a kitchen. | 人々は台所で料理をします。 |
| People eat in a dining room. | 人々はダイニングで食事をします。 |
| People wash in a bathroom. | 人々はバスルームで洗います。 |
| People read or write in a study. | 人々は書斎で読み書きをします。 |

新しい形容詞 sunny, comfortable, large, quiet, new も出てきましたね。

| Miami is a sunny city; London is not a sunny city. | マイアミは太陽がさんさんと注ぐ都市です。ロンドンは太陽がさんさんと注ぐ都市ではありません。 |
| A good chair or bed is comfortable. A bad chair or bed is not comfortable. | いい椅子やいいベッドは心地いいです。悪い椅子や悪いベッドは心地良くありません。 |
| Large is big. Do you have a large family or a small family? | Largeは大きいという意味です。あなたの家族は大家族ですか、それとも小家族ですか。 |
| A library is quiet. A big party is not quiet. A big party is loud. | 図書館は静かです。大きなパーティーは静かではありません。大きなパーティーはうるさいです。 |
| New is not old. New computers are good. | Newは古くないということです。新しいパソコンはいいです。 |

## ◉ Culture Note

裏庭 (backyard) は多くのアメリカ人にとって、とても重要なものです。裏庭で植物や野菜を育てたり、バーベキュー（肉や野菜を屋外で焼く）をしたり、遊んだりします。芝生 (lawn)の手入れもします。玄関にベランダがある家もあり、座ってリラックスできます。

Hello! How Are You?　　　Big or Small? Short or Tall?　　　Everyday Life

This Is My Family　　　　　Welcome to My Home

# Grammar Builder 1

▶ 4D Grammar Builder 1 (CD 1, Track 33)

## THE と A/AN

会話の中で初めて話題に出てきた事柄には冠詞の**a**をつけます。それ以降は**the**を使います。

| | |
|---|---|
| We live in a house.<br>The house has four bedrooms.<br>The house is big. | 私達は一軒家に住んでいます。<br>家には寝室が4つあります。<br>家は大きいです。 |
| There's a living room in the house.<br>The living room is comfortable.<br>But the living room is small. | 家には居間があります。<br>居間は心地良いです。<br>でも居間は狭いです。 |
| There's a dining room in the house.<br>The dining room is large.<br>The dining room is sunny. | 家にはダイニングがあります。<br>ダイニングは広いです。<br>ダイニングは日当たりがいいです。 |
| There's a study in the house.<br>The study is quiet.<br>There are books and a desk in the study. | 家には書斎があります。<br>書斎は静かです。<br>書斎には本と机があります。 |

a, e, i, o, u の音で始まる単語の前には a の代わりに an を使います。けれども the はこれらの音の前でもそのままです。

| | |
|---|---|
| I live in an apartment.<br>The apartment is very small. | アパートに住んでいます。<br>アパートはとても狭いです。 |
| There is an excellent professor at the university.<br>The professor's name is Mary Wheaton. | 大学には優秀な先生がいます。<br>先生の名前はメアリー・ウィートンです。 |

a や an は不定冠詞として、不特定のものに使われます。

| There is a new restaurant near the university. (Good? Bad? Italian? French? Thai? … ) | 大学の近くに新しいレストランがあります。 (いい？悪い？フレンチ？イタリアン？タイ料理？・・・) |
|---|---|
| There's a new computer in the study. (Sony? Dell? HP? … ) | 書斎に新しいパソコンがあります。 (ソニー？デル？ヒューレットパッカード？・・・) |
| A man is in the classroom. (A professor? A student? … ) | 教室に男の人がいます。 (先生？学生？・・・) |

the は定冠詞として特定のものに 使います。

| The new restaurant near the university is very good. | 大学の近くの新しいレストランはとてもいいです。 |
|---|---|
| The new computer in the study is a Sony. | 書斎の新しいパソコンはソニー製です。 |
| The man in the classroom is a new student. | 教室にいる男の人は新入生です。 |

the は誰もが知っている有名な物にも使います。特定な物だからです。

| The Statue of Liberty is in New York. | 自由の女神はニューヨークにあります。 |
|---|---|
| The Eiffel Tower is in Paris. | エッフェル塔はパリにあります。 |
| The White House is in Washington, D.C. | ホワイトハウスはワシントンDCにあります。 |
| The Taj Mahal is in India. | タージ・マハルはインドにあります。 |
| The Great Wall is in China. | 万里の長城は中国にあります。 |

Hello! How Are You?     Big or Small? Short or Tall?     Everyday Life

This Is My Family                    Welcome to My Home

## Vocabulary Builder 2

▶ 4E Vocabulary Builder 2 (CD 1, Track 34)

| | |
|---|---|
| I live in a small apartment. | 私は狭いアパートに住んでいます。 |
| In the living room there are two chairs, a couch, a bookshelf, and a television. | 居間には椅子が二つとソファーと本棚とテレビがあります。 |
| The couch is old, but the television is new. | ソファーは古いですが、テレビは新しいです。 |
| I have a refrigerator, a stove, a dishwasher, and a sink in the kitchen. | キッチンには冷蔵庫とコンロと食器洗い機と流し台があります。 |
| The dishwasher is old, but it's good. | 食器洗い機は古いですが、いいです。 |
| There is also a table with two chairs in the kitchen. | 台所にはテーブル一つと椅子二つがあります。 |
| The table is very small, but the chairs are comfortable. | テーブルはとても小さいですが、椅子は座り心地がいいです。 |
| There is a bed, a dresser, and a desk in my bedroom. | 私の寝室にはベッドとたんすと机があります。 |
| The dresser has my clothes in it. | たんすには洋服が入っています。 |
| Of course there's a bathroom in my apartment. | もちろん私のアパートにはバスルームがあります。 |
| The bathroom is very, very small! | バスルームはとてもとても狭いです! |
| The bathroom has a toilet and shower, but it doesn't have a bathtub. | バスルームにはトイレとシャワーがありますが、バスタブはありません。 |

# ✎ Vocabulary Practice 2

適切な答えを選んでください。

1. The couch is in the _____.

   a. bedroom

   b. dining room

   c. bathroom

   d. living room

2. The _____ is in the kitchen.

   a. couch

   b. sink

   c. toilet

   d. bed

3. The _____ is in the dining room.

   a. table

   b. toilet

   c. bed

   d. dresser

4. The _____ is in the study.

   a. toilet

   b. stove

   c. bookshelf

   d. bed

Hello! How Are You?          Big or Small? Short or Tall?          Everyday Life

This Is My Family                    Welcome to My Home

5.  The stove is in the _____.

    a. kitchen

    b. bedroom

    c. bathroom

    d. dining room

6.  There is a new _____ in the living room.

    a. shower

    b. refrigerator

    c. bed

    d. television

7.  The dishwasher is in the _____.

    a. dining room

    b. kitchen

    c. bedroom

    d. bathroom

8.  The _____ is in the bathroom.

    a. stove

    b. toilet

    c. couch

    d. bed

9. The _____ is in the bedroom.

   a. sink

   b. shower

   c. stove

   d. bed

10. The refrigerator is in the _____.

   a. living room

   b. dining room

   c. kitchen

   d. bedroom

11. The dresser is in the _____.

   a. bedroom

   b. kitchen

   c. dining room

   d. living room

12. The _____ is in the bathroom.

   a. stove

   b. couch

   c. television

   d. shower

   答え
   1. d; 2. b; 3. a; 4. c; 5. a; 6. d; 7. b; 8. b; 9. d; 10. c; 11. a; 12. d

Hello! How Are You?　　Big or Small? Short or Tall?　　Everyday Life

This Is My Family　　Welcome to My Home

# Grammar Builder 2

▶ 4F Grammar Builder 2 (CD 1, Track 35)

## 前置詞 IN, ON, UNDER など

よく使われる前置詞を見てみましょう。

**In（～に、～で、～の中に、～の中で）**

| We live in a house. | 私達は一軒家に住んでいます。 |
|---|---|
| Beijing is in China. | 北京は中国にあります。 |

**On（～の上に、～に）**

| The books are on the bookshelf. | 本は本棚にあります。 |
|---|---|
| The computer is on the desk. | パソコンは机の上です。 |

**From（～から、～出身）**

| Ram is from India. | ラムさんはインド出身です。 |
|---|---|
| John is from Boston. | ジョンさんはボストン出身です。 |

**Next to（～の隣）**

| The chair is next to the table. | 椅子はテーブルの隣です。 |
|---|---|
| New York is next to New Jersey. | ニューヨークはニュージャージーの隣です。 |

**Near（～の近く）**

| New York is near Philadelphia. | ニューヨークはフィラデルフィアの近くです。 |
|---|---|
| The restaurant is near the university. | レストランは大学の近くです。 |

Around Town | Let's Go Shopping | What Do You Feel Like Doing?

Let's Eat! | At Work

## Far from（〜から遠い）

| Los Angeles is far from New York. | ロサンゼルスはニューヨークから遠いです。 |
| South Africa is far from Japan. | 南アフリカは日本から遠いです。 |

## Under（〜の下）

| The cat is under the couch. | 猫はソファーの下にいます。 |
| The dog is under the table. | 犬はテーブルの下にいます。 |

## Between（〜の間）

| The bathroom is between the bedroom and the kitchen. | バスルームは寝室と台所の間です。 |
| New York is between Boston and Philadelphia. | ニューヨークはボストンとフィラデルフィアの間です。 |

# ✎ Work Out 1

▶ 4G Work Out 1 (CD 1, Track 36)

音声を聞いて空欄を埋めてください。

1. There's _____ under the bed.

2. _____ cat's name is Patches.

3. There is _____ very good student in the class.

4. _____ is from Chicago.

5. There is _____ excellent Thai restaurant _____ here.

6. _____ restaurant is _____ the university.

7. John has _____ computer.

Hello! How Are You?      Big or Small? Short or Tall?      Everyday Life

This Is My Family                    Welcome to My Home

8. _____ computer is _____ his desk.

9. They _____ in _____ apartment.

10. _____ is small, but comfortable.

**答え**

1. a cat; 2. The; 3. a; 4. The student; 5. an, near; 6. The, next to; 7. a new; 8. The, on; 9. live, an; 10. The apartment

## 🎧 Bring It All Together

▶ 4H Bring It All Together (CD 1, Track 37)

サラさんは新しいアパートに入居しました。友人のビルさんが初めてサラさんのアパートを訪れます。

| | |
|---|---|
| Bill: | Hey, Sarah! So, this is your new apartment? |
| ビル: | サラ！これが君の新しいアパート？ |
| Sarah: | Yes! Welcome to my new home! |
| サラ: | そうよ！私の新居へようこそ！ |
| Bill: | It's great. It's next to the university, and near really good restaurants. |
| ビル: | いいね。大学の隣だし、すごくいいレストランの近くだし。 |
| Sarah: | Yeah, it's fantastic. This is my living room. |
| サラ: | うん、素晴らしいわ。これが私の居間よ。 |
| Bill: | It's very sunny. And is that a new couch? |
| ビル: | とても日当たりがいいね。あれは新しいソファー？ |
| Sarah: | Yes, the couch is new. The chair is old, though. |
| サラ: | そう、ソファーは新しいわ。でも椅子は古いの。 |
| Bill: | But it's a comfortable chair. |
| ビル: | でも座り心地のいい椅子だね。 |
| Sarah: | Perfect for a good book. |
| サラ: | いい本を読むには最適ね。 |
| Bill: | Or good television! |

| | |
|---|---|
| ビル： | それか、いいテレビね！ |
| Sarah: | Yeah, that, too. |
| サラ： | うん、それもね。 |
| Bill: | How many bedrooms do you have? |
| ビル： | 寝室はいくつあるの？ |
| Sarah: | There are two bedrooms. One is my bedroom, and the other is my study. I have a desk and bookshelves in there. |
| サラ： | 寝室は二つ。一つは私の寝室で、もう一つは私の書斎にしてるの。机と本棚があるわ。 |
| Bill: | Where's your computer? |
| ビル： | パソコンはどこ？ |
| Sarah: | The computer is in the study. |
| サラ： | パソコンは書斎よ。 |
| Bill: | And that's your kitchen? |
| ビル： | それからあれは台所？ |
| Sarah: | Yeah, it's small and not very sunny. The refrigerator and stove are really old. And I don't have a dishwasher. |
| サラ： | うん、狭くてあまり日当たりがよくないの。冷蔵庫とコンロはすごく古い。それから食器洗い機もないの。 |
| Bill: | No problem! You've got great restaurants right here! And … the bathroom? |
| ビル： | 心配無用！すぐそこにいいレストランがあるよ！それから・・・バスルームは？ |
| Sarah: | It's very nice. |
| サラ： | とてもいいわ。 |
| Bill: | No, where's the bathroom? |
| ビル： | そうじゃなくて、バスルームはどこ？ |
| Sarah: | Oh! Right there, next to the bedroom. |
| サラ： | ああ！あそこよ、寝室のとなり。 |
| Bill: | Thanks. I'll be right back … |
| ビル： | ありがとう。すぐ戻るよ・・・ |

だいいっか 4: Welcome to My Home

Hello! How Are You?      Big or Small? Short or Tall?      Everyday Life

This Is My Family      Welcome to My Home

# ✎ Work Out 2

the, a, an のうち、適切な冠詞を空欄に埋めてください。

1. Mr. Archer is _____ man.

2. Jenny is _____ excellent student.

3. John has _____ dog. _____ dog's name is Lola.

4. _____ Taj Mahal is in India.

5. There is _____ really good restaurant near here.

6. I have _____ new computer. _____ computer is really good.

7. Do you have _____ brother?

8. Where is _____ Grand Canyon?

9. Sarah has _____ apartment. _____ apartment is small, but comfortable.

10. There's _____ desk in the study.

11. Are you taking _____ English literature class?

12. Yes, I'm taking _____ English literature class. _____ professor is excellent.

**答え**
1. a; 2. an; 3. a, The; 4. The; 5. a; 6. a, The; 7. a; 8. the; 9. an, The; 10. a; 11. an; 12. an, The

適切な前置詞を選んでください。

1. John is (in/on) his bedroom.

2. There is a book (on/between) the desk.

3. The bathroom is (from/next to) the bedroom.

4. Cape Town is (near/far from) Tokyo.

5. The dog is (under/in) the table.

6. Billy is (from/between) his mother and his father.

7. Yukiko is (from/on) Osaka.

8. London is (on/in) the United Kingdom.

9. There is a good Thai restaurant (near/under) the university.

10. There are twenty students (in/from) the class.

   **答え**
   1. in; 2. on; 3. next to; 4. far from; 5. under; 6. between; 7. from; 8. in; 9. near; 10. in

## ✎ Drive It Home

**the, a, an** の復習をしましょう。まずは空欄に **a** か **an** のどちらかを埋めてください。

1. There is _____ new student in the class.

2. There is _____ excellent restaurant near the university.

3. There is _____ good book on my desk.

4. There is _____ dining room in the house.

   **答え**
   1. a; 2. an; 3. a; 4. a

それぞれの空欄に **the** を入れてください。

1. There is a new student in the class. _____ student is from Chicago.

Hello! How Are You?        Big or Small? Short or Tall?        Everyday Life

This Is My Family                    Welcome to My Home

2. There is an excellent restaurant near the university. _____ restaurant is new.

3. There is a good book on my desk. _____ book is War and Peace.

4. There is a dining room in the house. _____ dining room is not very big.

**答え**
1. The; 2. The; 3. The; 4. The

## Parting Words

**Well done!**（よくできました！）第4課はこれで終了です。学習した内容を確認してみましょう。

☐ 家やアパートの各部屋の名前　（まだ自信がない場合は p.61 に戻って復習しましょう。）

☐ **the** と **a/an**　（まだ自信がない場合は p.64 に戻って復習しましょう。）

☐ 家やアパートにある物の名前　（まだ自信がない場合は p.66 に戻って復習しましょう。）

☐ **in, on, under** といった前置詞　（まだ自信がない場合は p.70 に戻って復習しましょう。）

☐ 自分の家について説明する　（まだ自信がない場合は p.72 に戻って復習しましょう。）

## Take It Further

▶ 4l Bring It All Together (CD 1, Track 38)

**one** から **one hundred** までの数はもう分かりますね。今度は **first, second, third** といった序数を見てみましょう。

| first, second, third, fourth | 一番目、二番目、三番目、四番目 |
|---|---|
| fifth, sixth, seventh, eighth | 五番目、六番目、七番目、八番目 |

| ninth, tenth, eleventh, twelfth | 九番目、十番目、十一番目、十二番目 |
| This is the fourth lesson of Essential English. | これはEssential Englishの第4課です。 |
| January is the first month of the year. | 一月は一年の最初の月です。 |
| February is the second month of the year. | 二月は一年の二番目の月です。 |
| Thursday is the fourth day of the work week. | 木曜日は四番目の平日です。 |

www.livinglanguage.com/languagelab のページをチェック
するのを忘れずに。バーチャル単語帳やゲームやクイズで、学習
したことを復習してみましょう!

# Word Recall

本課で学習した単語を覚えているか確認してみましょう。

1. What is not in the kitchen?

   a. the sink

   b. the refrigerator

   c. a bed

   d. a table

2. What is not in the living room?

   a. a television

   b. a couch

   c. a chair

   d. the shower

3. What is not in the bedroom?

   a. a sink

   b. a bed

   c. a dresser

   d. a chair

4. What is not in the bathroom?

   a. the toilet

   b. the stove

**Essential English**

c. the shower

d. the sink

5. **What is not in the study?**

a. a chair

b. a desk

c. the dishwasher

d. the computer

Hello! How Are You?　　　　　Big or Small? Short or Tall?　　　　　Everyday Life

This Is My Family　　　　　Welcome to My Home

# だいいっか 5: 毎日の生活

## Lesson 5: Everyday Life

本課では日常生活について話します。レッスン内容は以下の通りです。

□ 曜日

□ 時間

□ 日常生活の行動を表す動詞

□ 動詞の現在形

□ 一日の過ごし方についての会話の中で、学習した項目を総合的に使う
　さあ始めましょう!

# Vocabulary Builder 1

▶ 5A Vocabulary Builder 1 (CD 2, Track 1)

| | |
|---|---|
| I wake up at seven o'clock in the morning. | 私は朝7時に起きます。 |
| I brush my teeth and take a shower. | 私は歯を磨いてシャワーを浴びます。 |
| I get dressed. | 私は洋服を着ます。 |
| I eat breakfast./I have breakfast. | 私は朝ご飯を食べます。 |
| I read the newspaper. | 私は新聞を読みます。 |
| I go to work at eight thirty. | 私は8時30分に仕事に行きます。 |
| I take the train to my office. | 私は電車に乗って会社に行きます。 |
| I work from nine o'clock until six o'clock. | 私は9時から6時まで仕事をします。 |
| I eat/have lunch at twelve thirty in the afternoon. | 私は午後12時30分に昼ご飯を食べます。 |
| I leave work at six o'clock in the evening. | 私は夕方6時に会社を出ます。 |
| I get home at six thirty. | 私は6時30分に帰宅します。 |
| I eat/have dinner with my family at seven o'clock. | 私は7時に家族と一緒に夕飯を食べます。 |
| During dinner we talk about our day. | 夕飯の間、私達はその日一日について話します。 |
| After dinner we do the dishes and then watch television. | 夕飯の後、私達は皿を洗い、そしてテレビを見ます。 |
| The kids do their homework and listen to music. | 子供達は宿題をして音楽を聞きます。 |
| My wife and I read before bed. | 妻と私は寝る前に読書をします。 |
| We go to sleep at eleven thirty at night. | 私達は夜11時30分に寝ます。 |

Hello! How Are You?　　Big or Small? Short or Tall?　　Everyday Life

This Is My Family　　Welcome to My Home

# ✎ Vocabulary Practice 1

⏵ 5B Vocabulary Practice 1 (CD 2, Track 2)

ボキャブラリーの練習です。音声を聞いて空欄を適切な動詞で埋めてください。

1. I _____ up at 7:00 in the morning.

2. I _____ my teeth and _____ a shower.

3. I _____ dressed.

4. I _____ breakfast.

5. I _____ the newspaper.

6. I _____ to work at 8:30.

7. I _____ the train to my office.

8. I _____ from 9:00 until 6:00.

9. I _____ lunch at 12:30 in the afternoon.

10. I _____ work at 6:00 in the evening.

11. I _____ home at 6:30.

12. I _____ dinner with my family at 7:00.

13. During dinner we _____ about our day.

14. After dinner we _____ the dishes and then _____ television.

15. The kids _____ their homework and _____ to music.

16. My wife and I _____ before bed.

17. We _____ to sleep at 11:30 at night.

**答え**

1. wake; 2. brush, take; 3. get; 4. eat/have; 5. read; 6. go; 7. take; 8. work; 9. eat/have; 10. leave; 11. get; 12. eat/have; 13. talk; 14. do, watch; 15. do, listen; 16. read; 17. go

---

# Take It Further

▶ 5C Take It Further (CD 2, Track 3)

曜日の言い方を見てみましょう。

| Monday | 月曜日 |
|--------|--------|
| Tuesday | 火曜日 |
| Wednesday | 水曜日 |
| Thursday | 木曜日 |
| Friday | 金曜日 |
| Saturday | 土曜日 |
| Sunday | 日曜日 |

| There are seven days in a week. | 一週間は七日です。 |
|---------------------------------|-------------------|
| The work week has five days. | 平日は五日間です。 |
| Monday is the first day of the work week. | 月曜日は平日の最初の日です。 |
| There are two days in the weekend: Saturday and Sunday. | 週末は二日間あります。土曜日と日曜日です。 |

動詞 start (始まる) と end (終わる)、そして before (〜の前), during (〜の間), after (〜の後) を見てみましょう。

| The work week starts on Monday. | 平日は月曜日から始まります。 |
|---------------------------------|------------------------------|
| The work week ends on Friday. | 平日は金曜日に終わります。 |
| Monday is before Tuesday. | 月曜日は火曜日の前です。 |
| Wednesday is after Tuesday. | 水曜日は火曜日の後です。 |

Hello! How Are You?          Big or Small? Short or Tall?          Everyday Life

This Is My Family                        Welcome to My Home

| Tuesday and Wednesday are during the work week. | 火曜日と水曜日は平日です。 |

# Grammar Builder 1
▶ 5D Grammar Builder 1 (CD 2, Track 4)

**時間**

**What time is it?**（今何時ですか。）「〜時」と言うには数字に **o'clock** をつけます。

| It's one o'clock. | 時です。 |
| It's seven o'clock. | 時です。 |

**thirty** は「30分」、**half past** は「半」です。

| It's five thirty.<br>It's half past five. | 時30分です。<br>時半です。 |
| It's ten thirty.<br>It's half past ten. | 時30分です。<br><br>時半です。 |

「15分」と言うには **fifteen** か **quarter past** か **quarter after** を使います。**a quarter past** の **a** は付けても付けなくても大丈夫です。

| It's four fifteen.<br>It's (a) quarter past four.<br>It's (a) quarter after four. | 4時15分です。 |
| It's eight fifteen.<br>It's (a) quarter past eight.<br>It's (a) quarter after eight. | 8時15分です。 |

「45分」は **forty-five** と言うか、**quarter to** を使って「〜時15分前」と言います。

| | |
|---|---|
| It's nine forty-five. | 9時45分です。 |
| It's (a) quarter to ten. | 10時15分前です。 |
| It's two forty-five. | 2時45分です。 |
| It's (a) quarter to three. | 3時15分前です。 |

その他の時間を言う時は数字をそのまま使います。

| | |
|---|---|
| It's one twenty. | 1時20分です。 |
| It's three twenty-five. | 3時25分です。 |
| It's six fifty-five. | 6時55分です。 |

**after/past**（〜分過ぎ）か **to**（〜分前）を使うこともできます。

| | |
|---|---|
| It's twenty after two.<br>It's twenty past two. | 2時20分（過ぎ）です。 |
| It's ten after three.<br>It's ten past three. | 3時10分（過ぎ）です。 |
| It's twenty to seven. | 7時20分前です。 |
| It's ten to nine. | 9時10分前です。 |

その他の時刻を表す表現です。

| | |
|---|---|
| It's noon. | 昼の12時です。 |
| It's midnight. | 夜の12時です。 |
| It's nine in the morning. | 朝9時です。 |
| It's three in the afternoon. | 午後3時です。 |
| It's six in the evening. | 夕方6時です。 |
| It's ten at night. | 夜10時です。 |

Hello! How Are You?    Big or Small? Short or Tall?    Everyday Life

This Is My Family    Welcome to My Home

morning, afternoon, evening, night の代わりに a.m. や p.m. を使うこともできます。

| It's nine thirty a.m. | 午前9時30分です。 |
|---|---|
| It's three p.m. | 午後3時です。 |
| It's six forty-five p.m. | 午後6時45分です。 |
| It's ten p.m. | 午後10時です。 |

質問するには what time を使い、答えるには at を使います。

| What time do you wake up? | あなたは何時に起きますか。 |
|---|---|
| I wake up at seven thirty in the morning. | 私は朝7時30分に起きます。 |
| What time do you have dinner? | あなた達は何時に夕飯を食べますか。 |
| We have dinner at seven thirty in the evening. | 私達は夜7時30分に夕飯を食べます。 |

## Vocabulary Builder 2

▶ 5E Vocabulary Builder 2 (CD 2, Track 5)

| During the week, John wakes up early for work. | 平日はジョンさんは仕事のために早く起きます。 |
|---|---|
| But on the weekend, he sleeps late. | でも週末は彼は遅くまで寝ます。 |
| He gets up at nine thirty. | 彼は9時30分に起きます。 |
| He watches TV while he eats/has breakfast. | 彼は朝ご飯を食べながらテレビを見ます。 |
| Then he goes to the gym. | それから彼はジムに行きます。 |
| After the gym, John goes running in the park. | ジムの後、ジョンさんは公園へ走りに行きます。 |
| In the afternoon, John reads magazines or uses the computer. | 午後にジョンさんは雑誌を読むかパソコンを使います。 |

| He reads and writes e-mails to his friends and family. | 彼は友人や家族とのメールを読み書きします。 |
| On Saturday nights, John sees his friends. | 土曜の夜、ジョンさんは友人に会います。 |
| They go to a restaurant or to the movies. | 彼らはレストランか映画に行きます。 |
| John gets home late on Saturday nights. | ジョンさんは土曜の夜は遅く帰宅します。 |
| He goes to bed after midnight or at one o'clock in the morning. | 彼は夜12時過ぎか午前1時に寝ます。 |
| On Sunday mornings, John stays in bed until ten o'clock. | 日曜の朝、ジョンさんは10時までベッドにいます。 |
| John works hard during the week, but he relaxes on the weekend. | ジョンさんは平日は一生懸命働きますが、週末はリラックスします。 |

# ✎ Vocabulary Practice 2

▶ 5F Vocabulary Practice 2 (CD 2, Track 6)

音声を聞いて空欄を適切な動詞で埋めてください。

1. During the week, John _____ up early for work.

2. But on the weekend, he _____ late.

3. He _____ up at nine thirty.

4. He _____ TV while he _____ breakfast.

5. Then he _____ to the gym.

6. After the gym, John _____ running in the park.

Hello! How Are You?    Big or Small? Short or Tall?    Everyday Life

This Is My Family    Welcome to My Home

7. In the afternoon, John _____ magazines or _____ the computer.

8. He _____ and _____ e-mails to his friends and family.

9. On Saturday nights, John _____ his friends.

10. They _____ to a restaurant or to the movies.

11. John _____ home late on Saturday nights.

12. He _____ to bed after midnight or one o'clock in the morning.

13. On Sunday mornings, John _____ in bed until ten o'clock.

14. John _____ hard during the week, but he _____ on the weekend.

**答え**
1. wakes; 2. sleeps; 3. gets; 4. watches, eats/has; 5. goes; 6. goes; 7. reads, uses; 8. reads, writes, 9. sees; 10. go; 11. gets; 12. goes; 13. stays; 14. works, relaxes

# Grammar Builder 2
▶ 5G Grammar Builder 2 (CD 2, Track 7)

### 動詞の現在形

現在形では he, she, it が主語の場合は動詞の語尾に –s か –es を付けます。ほとんどの動詞では –s を付けます。

| I work<br>私は働きます | we work<br>私達は働きます |
|---|---|
| you work<br>あなたは働きます | you work<br>あなた達は働きます |

| he, she, it works<br>彼は働きます、彼女は働きます、それは働きます | they work<br>彼ら/彼女ら/それらは働きます |
|---|---|

| I work at the university. | 私は大学で働きます。 |
|---|---|
| We see our friends on the weekend. | 私達は週末に友人に会います。 |
| Mary reads e-mail on her computer. | メアリーさんはパソコンでメールを読みます。 |
| They get home very late on Saturday nights. | 彼らは土曜の夜はとても遅く帰宅します。 |

he, she, it が主語の時、–ch, –sh, –x, –z, –s で終わる動詞には語尾に –es を付けます。

| He watches TV at night. | 彼は夜テレビを見ます。 |
|---|---|
| She relaxes on the weekend. | 彼女は週末にリラックスします。 |
| John brushes his teeth before he takes a shower. | ジョンさんはシャワーを浴びる前に歯を磨きます。 |

–o で終わる動詞にも –es を付けますが、発音の違いに注意してください。

| The student does her homework. | 学生は宿題をします。 |
|---|---|
| Jack goes to the movies with his friends. | ジャックさんは友人と映画に行きます。 |

–y で終わる名詞を複数形にする時は語尾を –ies に変えますね。例えば city の複数形は cities、university の複数形は universities です。–y で終わる動詞には、主語が he, she, it の時、語尾を –ies にします。

| John studies English literature at the university. | ジョンさんは大学で英文学を勉強します。 |
|---|---|

Hello! How Are You?          Big or Small? Short or Tall?          **Everyday Life**

This Is My Family          Welcome to My Home

# ✎ Work Out 1

▶ 5H Work Out 1 (CD 2, Track 8)

音声を聞いて適切な形の動詞を空欄に埋めてください。

1. It _____ Saturday, so John _____ in bed late.

2. On Monday, we _____ up early and _____ to work.

3. Professor Wheaton _____ twenty three students. They _____ English literature.

4. Peter _____ the computer in the evening.

5. He _____ e-mails and _____ the newspaper.

6. Mr. Archer _____ with his family on the weekend.

7. People _____ the train or the bus to work.

8. I _____ home at six o'clock in the evening.

9. Sarah _____ lunch and _____ TV.

10. The children _____ in their bedroom.

11. We _____ to the movies on Friday night and _____ home on Saturday night.

12. Joe _____ up and _____ his teeth.

13. You _____ to music and _____ your homework.

14. The students _____ to their professor.

**答え**

1. is, stays; 2. get, go; 3. has, study; 4. uses; 5. writes, reads; 6. relaxes; 7. take; 8. get; 9. eats/ has, watches; 10. sleep; 11. go, stay; 12. gets, brushes; 13. listen, do; 14. talk

**Essential English**

## 🔊 Bring It All Together
▶ 5I Bring It All Together (CD 2, Track 9)

本課で学習した項目を盛り込んだ会話の練習です。ボブさんとスーザンさんはスーパーにいます。二人の話を聞いてみましょう。

| | |
|---|---|
| Bob: | Hey, Susan. How's it going? |
| ボブ： | あ、スーザン。元気？ |
| Susan: | Hi Bob! Good to see you. What's new? How are Diana and the kids? |
| スーザン： | こんにちは、ボブ！会えて嬉しいわ。最近どう？ダイアナとお子さんは元気？ |
| Bob: | They're good. Diana has a new job, and the kids are in school. |
| ボブ： | 元気だよ。ダイアナは新しい仕事に就いて、子供達は学校に行ってるよ。 |
| Susan: | A new job? That's great. But today is Friday. You're not at the office? |
| スーザン： | 新しい仕事？それは良かったわね。でも今日は金曜日よ。あなたは会社じゃないの？ |
| Bob: | Oh, no, I don't work on Fridays. I have Fridays off. |
| ボブ： | ああ、いや、僕は金曜は仕事に行かないんだ。金曜日は休み。 |
| Susan: | You have Fridays off? A three-day weekend every week? Lucky you! |
| スーザン： | 金曜が休みなの？毎週三連休？羨ましいわ！ |
| Bob: | Yeah, it's great. Diana goes to work, the kids go to school, and I stay home and do nothing! |
| ボブ： | うん、いいものだよ。ダイアナは仕事だし、子供達は学校だし、僕は家で何もしないんだ！ |
| Susan: | Come on, Bob. That's not true. You're here at the supermarket! |
| スーザン： | 何言ってるのボブ。そんなことないでしょ。スーパーに来てるじゃない！ |
| Bob: | You're right. After I bring the kids to school, I come to the supermarket and buy food for the family for the weekend. |

だいいっか 5: Everyday Life    **91**

Hello! How Are You?　　　　Big or Small? Short or Tall?　　　　Everyday Life

This Is My Family　　　　Welcome to My Home

| ボブ： | まあそうだね。子供達を学校に送ってからスーパーに来て家族の週末の食料を買うんだ。 |
| --- | --- |
| Susan: | So, you bring the kids to school, and then go food shopping. |
| スーザン： | 子供さんを学校に送って、それから食料品の買出しに行くのね。 |
| Bob: | Well, after I bring the kids to school, I go to the post office. |
| ボブ： | えっと、子供達を学校に送った後で、郵便局に行くんだ。 |
| Susan: | And after you go food shopping, you go home and relax? |
| スーザン： | それから食料品の買出しの後、家に帰ってリラックスするの？ |
| Bob: | Um, no, not really. After I go food shopping I go home and clean the house. |
| ボブ： | うーん、いや、そういうわけでもないんだ。食料品の買い物をした後、家に帰って掃除をするんだ。 |
| Susan: | And then you relax? You read or watch television? |
| スーザン： | それからリラックスするの？本を読んだりテレビを見たり？ |
| Bob: | No, then I do laundry. |
| ボブ： | いや、それから洗濯をするんだ。 |
| Susan: | And after you do laundry, you relax? |
| スーザン： | それで洗濯をした後でリラックスするの？ |
| Bob: | No, then I start to cook, and after that, I … |
| ボブ： | いや、それから料理を始めるんだ、それでその後で僕は・・・ |
| Susan: | Bob, you don't have a three-day weekend. You don't have Fridays off. |
| スーザン： | ボブ、あなたは三連休なんかじゃないわね。金曜日はお休みじゃないわ。 |
| Bob: | I don't? |
| ボブ： | そう？ |
| Susan: | No, you work a lot on Fridays. |
| スーザン： | ええ、あなたは金曜日にたくさん働いてるわ。 |
| Bob: | Hmm. I think you're right! |
| ボブ： | うーん。確かに君は正しいかも！ |
| Susan: | Well, Bob, enjoy the rest of your "day off"! |
| スーザン： | じゃあボブ、残りの「休日」を楽しんでね！ |

**Essential English**

| Bob: | Gee, thanks a lot, Susan! |
| ボブ: | うわあ、スーザンどうもありがとう! |

## Take It Further

▶ 5J Take It Further (CD 2, Track 10)

動詞 **have** を否定文で使うには **do** か **does** を一緒に使います。

| I have a big family. | 私の家族は大家族です。 |
| I do not have a big family.<br>I don't have a big family. | 私の家族は大家族ではありません。 |
| She has a little brother. | 彼女は弟さんがいます。 |
| She does not have a little brother.<br>She doesn't have a little brother. | 彼女は弟さんがいません。 |

その他の一般動詞 (**work**, **relax**, **stay** など) も否定文では **do** か **does** を使います。

| Bob works on Thursdays.<br>Bob doesn't work on Fridays. | ボブさんは木曜日に働きます。<br>ボブさんは金曜日は働きません。 |
| Joan relaxes on the weekend.<br>Joan doesn't relax during the week. | ジョーンさんは週末にリラックスします。<br>ジョーンさんは平日はリラックスしません。 |
| Diana and Bob stay home on Saturdays.<br>They don't stay home on Mondays. | ダイアナさんとボブさんは土曜日に家にいます。<br>彼らは月曜日は家にいません。 |

**he, she, it** が主語の時、**–s/–es** が付く位置の違いに気づきましたか? 肯定文の場合は 本動詞の後に付きます。

| Bob works. | ボブさんは働きます。 |
| Joan relaxes. | ジョーンさんはリラックスします。 |

けれども、否定文の場合は **do** の後に **–es** が付きます。本動詞には付きません。

| Bob does not work. | ボブさんは働きません。 |

Hello! How Are You?          Big or Small? Short or Tall?          Everyday Life

This Is My Family                          Welcome to My Home

| Joan does not relax. | ジョーンさんはリラックスしません。 |

否定文中や疑問文中の **do** と **does** については第6課でもっと詳しく学習します。

## ✎ Work Out 2

時間を言う練習です。**What time is it?** の質問に答えてください。

例: 1:00
答え: **It's one o'clock.**

1. 9:00 _____

2. 10:15 _____

3. 8:30 _____

4. 7:45 _____

5. 12:00 p.m. _____

6. 12:00 a.m. _____

7. 2:10 _____

8. 4:20 _____

9. 10:40 _____

10. 6:55 _____

**答え**
1. It's nine o'clock. 2. It's ten fifteen./It's (a) quarter past ten./It's (a) quarter after ten. 3. It's eight thirty./It's half past eight. 4. It's seven forty-five./It's (a) quarter to eight. 5. It's twelve o'clock in the afternoon./It's noon. 6. It's twelve o'clock (at night)./It's midnight. 7. It's two ten./It's ten past two./It's ten after two. 8. It's four twenty./It's twenty after four./It's twenty past

Around Town | Let's Go Shopping | What Do You Feel Like Doing?

Let's Eat! | At Work

four. 9. It's ten forty./It's twenty to eleven. 10. It's six fifty-five./It's five to seven.

よくできました。今度は正しい動詞の形を選んでください。

1. Brad (wake/wakes) up very early in the morning.

2. They (eat/eats) at a Thai restaurant on Saturdays.

3. I (work/works) from Monday to Friday.

4. Their professor doesn't (work/works) on Sundays.

5. Miriam (leave/leaves) the office at 5:30.

6. The boy (get/gets) dressed and then (eat/eats) breakfast.

7. We (have/has) dinner before we (watch/watches) television.

8. You (take/takes) the train to work.

9. My sister doesn't (listen/listens) to music while she (do/does) homework.

10. Bob (relax/relaxes) during the weekend, but doesn't (relax/relaxes) during

the week.

**答え**

1. wakes; 2. eat; 3. work; 4. work; 5. leaves; 6. gets, eats; 7. have, watch; 8. take; 9. listen, does;
10. relaxes, relax

## ✎ Drive It Home

指定された主語を使って各文を書き直してください。

1. We wake up early on Mondays. (He … )

_____

Hello! How Are You?   Big or Small? Short or Tall?   Everyday Life

This Is My Family   Welcome to My Home

2. I eat breakfast at nine thirty in the morning. (Susan ...)

_____

3. You take the bus to work. (Bill ...)

_____

4. They have lunch at twelve thirty in the afternoon. (Mrs. Ramirez ...)

_____

5. I work at the university. (The professor ...)

_____

6. We watch television after we eat dinner. (She ...)

_____

7. The boys brush their teeth before bed. (The boy ...)

_____

8. They go to bed early during the week. (John ...)

_____

**答え**
1. He wakes up early on Mondays. 2. Susan eats breakfast at nine thirty in the morning. 3. Bill takes the bus to work. 4. Mrs. Ramirez has lunch at twelve thirty in the afternoon. 5. The professor works at the university. 6. She watches television after she eats dinner. 7. The boy brushes his teeth before bed. 8. John goes to bed early during the week.

## Parting Words

**Congratulations!**(おめでとうございます!)また一つ Essential English のレッスンが終了しました。学習した内容を確認してみましょう。

☐ 曜日 (まだ自信がない場合は p.83 に戻って復習しましょう。)

☐ 時間 (まだ自信がない場合は p.84 に戻って復習しましょう。)

☐ 日常生活の行動を表す動詞 (まだ自信がない場合は p.86 に戻って復習しましょう。)

☐ 動詞の現在形 (まだ自信がない場合は p.88 に戻って復習しましょう。)

☐ 一日の過ごし方についての会話の中で、学習した項目を総合的に使う (まだ自信がない場合は p.91 に戻って復習しましょう。)

www.livinglanguage.com/languagelab のページをチェックするのを忘れずに。バーチャル単語帳やゲームやクイズで、学習したことを復習してみましょう!

# Word Recall

適切な動詞を選んでください。

1. I (wake/take/have) up very early during the week.

2. She (washes/does/brushes) her teeth.

3. You (do/take/make) a shower in the morning.

4. Bill (does/gets/takes) dressed after his shower.

5. They (read/write/eat) the newspaper every morning.

6. Professor Wheaton (goes/takes/does) to work at ten in the morning.

7. You (go/take/watch) the train to your office.

8. Bob (works/relaxes/sleeps) in his office from nine o'clock until six o'clock.

9. They (go/leave/take) work at six o'clock in the evening.

10. Mary (works/does/gets) home at seven in the evening.

11. We (have/do/read) dinner with friends at a restaurant.

12. He (makes/talks/writes) with his wife about his day.

13. The kids (watch/listen/read) television after their homework.

14. We (have/do/take) the dishes in the sink.

15. They (have/do/go) to sleep early during the week.

**答え**
1. wake; 2. brushes; 3. take; 4. gets; 5. read; 6. goes; 7. take; 8. works; 9. leave; 10. gets; 11. have; 12. talks; 13. watch; 14. do; 15. go

**Essential English**

# テスト1

## Quiz 1

第1課から第5課までで学習した内容をテスト形式で確認してみましょう。問題を解き終わったら自己採点をしてみてください。見直すべき箇所が見つかったら第6課に進む前に復習をしてください。
第10課の後にも復習テストが設けられています。その後は五つのまとめの会話、そして会話の内容を尋ねる問題で本書は締めくくられます。
それでは復習テストを始めましょう!

A. 適切な部屋を選んでください。

1. The sink is in …
2. The bed is in …
3. The couch is in …
4. The table and chairs are in …
5. The shower is in …

a. the bedroom.
b. the dining room.
c. the bathroom.
d. the kitchen.
e. the living room.

B. 複数形を書いてください。

1. one boy, two _____

2. one room, three _____

3. one woman, four _____

4. one city, five _____

5. one child, three _____

C. am, is, are, have, has の中から適切な単語を選んで空欄に埋めてください。

これで本書の半分が終わりました!おめでとうございます!

1. They _____ a small house.

2. _____ you the new professor?

3. Mary _____ in her bedroom.

4. Richard _____ three children.

5. I _____ American.

D. 正しい動詞の形を選んでください。

1. We (watch/watches) television every night.

2. Greg (relax/relaxes) during the weekend.

3. You (take/takes) the train to work.

4. She doesn't (works/work) in an office.

5. They (doesn't/don't) have dinner before six thirty.

E. Complete the sentences with the, a, or an.

1. There is _____ new professor at the university.

2. I have a dog. _____ dog's name is Max.

3. _____ Eiffel Tower is in Paris.

4. Marjorie is _____ excellent student.

5. Do you have _____ question?

**答え**
A. 1. d; 2. a; 3. e; 4. b; 5. c
B. 1. boys; 2. rooms; 3. women; 4. cities; 5. children
C. 1. have; 2. Are; 3. is; 4. has; 5. am
D. 1. watch; 2. relaxes; 3. take; 4. work; 5. don't
E. 1. a; 2. The; 3. The; 4. an; 5. a

# How Did You Do?

正解一つにつき一点として総合得点を出してみましょう。以下は、得点に応じたアドバイスです。

**0-10 点:** もう一度第1課から戻り、理解を確かめながら進めていくのがよいかもしれません。急ぐ必要は全くないですよ!あわてずに各課のボキャブラリーや文法項目を注意深く見ていきましょう。

**11-18 点:** セクション A の問題を間違えた場合はボキャブラリーの項目に戻って復習するとよいでしょう。セクション B, C, D, E の問題を間違えた場合は Grammar Builder に戻って文法の基礎をもう一度確認しましょう。

**19-25 点:** 第6課に進んでください。これまでの学習内容がしっかり頭に入っています!

点

これで本書の半分が終わりました!おめでとうございます!

Hello! How Are You?          Big or Small? Short or Tall?          Everyday Life

This Is My Family          Welcome to My Home

# だいいっか 6: 町で

## Lesson 6: Around Town

**Welcome back!** （またお会いしましたね！）本課では様々な場所についての話題を扱います。レッスン内容は以下の通りです。

☐ **town** や **city** にある色々な場所に関する基礎的な語彙

☐ **do** と **does** を含む疑問文と否定文

☐ 場所に関する更なる語彙

☐ 疑問詞

☐ 学習した項目を使って会話をする
それではまずは新しいボキャブラリーから始めましょう。

Around Town | Let's Go Shopping | What Do You Feel Like Doing?

Let's Eat! | At Work

# Vocabulary Builder 1

6A Vocabulary Builder 1 (CD 2, Track 11)

| Where is the bank? | 銀行はどこですか。 |
|---|---|
| The bank is on Main Street. | 銀行はメイン・ストリートにあります。 |
| There is an ATM in front of the bank. | 銀行の前にATMがあります。 |
| People get money at the ATM. | 人々はATMでお金をおろします。 |
| Across the street from the bank is the post office. | 銀行の向かい側に郵便局があります。 |
| People buy stamps and mail letters at the post office. | 人々は郵便局で切手を買ったり手紙を出したりします。 |
| Next to the post office is a small grocery store. | 郵便局の隣は小さい食料品店です。 |
| People buy food at the grocery store. | 人々は食料品店で食べ物を買います。 |
| Down the street there is a clothing store. | 道を少し行くと服屋があります。 |
| People buy clothes there. | 人々はそこで服を買います。 |
| There's a restaurant near the clothing store. | 服屋の近くにレストランがあります。 |
| And there's a gas station with a convenience store on Main Street. | それからメイン・ストリートにはコンビニ付きのガソリンスタンドがあります。 |
| People get gas for their cars at the gas station. | 人々はガソリンスタンドで車のガソリンを入れます。 |
| They buy coffee, newspapers, and magazines at the convenience store. | 彼らはコンビニでコーヒーや新聞や雑誌を買います。 |

Hello! How Are You?          Big or Small? Short or Tall?          Everyday Life

This Is My Family                    Welcome to My Home

# ✎ Vocabulary Practice 1

ボキャブラリーの練習をしましょう。**Where do you ...**

1. ... buy stamps and mail letters?     a. At a bank.

2. ... get money?     b. At a clothing store.

3. ... get gas and newspapers?     c. At a post office.

4. ... buy food?     d. At a restaurant.

5. ... eat dinner?     e. At a convenience store.

6. ... buy clothes?     f. At a grocery store.

**答え**
1. c; 2. a; 3. e; 4. f; 5.d; 6. b

町について話す時に出てくる動詞の練習をしてみましょう。

1. People _____ money at a bank or an ATM.

2. People _____ letters at the post office.

3. People _____ food at a grocery store and clothes at a clothing store.

4. People _____ gas for their cars at the gas station.

**答え**
1. get; 2. mail; 3. buy; 4. get/buy

# Take It Further

▶ 6B Take It Further 1 (CD 2, Track 12)

**GET**

動詞 get は色々な所で出てきましたが、ここでまとめて見てみましょう。

| I get dressed after I shower. | シャワーをした後で洋服を着ます。 |
| I get undressed before I go to bed. | 寝る前に洋服を脱ぎます。 |

**Essential English**

**Get (to)** は場所を表す言葉と一緒に使われると **arrive at**（着く）や **go to**（行く）という意味を持ちます。

| | |
|---|---|
| Bill gets to the office at nine o'clock in the morning. | ビルさんは朝9時に会社に着きます。 |
| The students get to class at one o'clock in the afternoon. | 学生は午後1時に授業に行きます。 |
| How do you get to work? By car or by train? | どうやって仕事に行きますか。車でですかそれとも電車でですか。 |
| Mary gets home at six in the evening. | メアリーさんは夕方6時に帰宅します。 |

**Get** には **to buy**（買う）や **to obtain**（入手する）という意味もあります。

| | |
|---|---|
| People get money at the ATM. | 人々はATMでお金をおろします。 |
| John gets gas at the gas station. | ジョンさんはガソリンスタンドでガソリンを入れます。 |
| You get newspapers and magazines at the convenience store. | あなたはコンビニで新聞や雑誌を買います。 |

**Get** には **become**（なる）という意味もあります。

| | |
|---|---|
| The children get sleepy at nine o'clock, and then they go to bed. | 子供達は9時に眠くなって寝ます。 |
| In Boston, the days get cold in December. | ボストンでは12月に寒くなります。 |
| The days get hot in August. | 八月に暑くなります。 |

**Get** は英語でよく使われる動詞です。これから先のレッスンでもこの動詞についてもっと見ていきます。

Hello! How Are You?    Big or Small? Short or Tall?    Everyday Life

This Is My Family    Welcome to My Home

# Grammar Builder 1

▶ 6C Grammar Builder 1 (CD 2, Track 13)

## DO と DOES

be 動詞以外の動詞を否定形 にするには do (主語が I, you, we, they の時) か
does (主語が he, she, it の時) を使います。Do + not は don't と短縮され、does +
not は doesn't と短縮されます。

| | |
|---|---|
| You work at a bank. <br> You do not work at a bank. <br> You don't work at a bank. | あなたは銀行で働きます。 <br> あなたは銀行では働きません。 |
| We eat dinner at the restaurant. <br> We do not eat dinner at the restaurant. <br> We don't eat dinner at the restaurant. | 私達はレストランで夕飯を食べます。 <br> 私達はレストランでは夕食を食べません。 |

肯定文の主語が he, she, it の場合は、takes, goes, fixes のように動詞の語尾が
–s か –es になりますね。けれども否定文では本動詞に –s や –es が付くのではな
く、doesn't take, doesn't go, doesn't fix といったように does を使います。

| | |
|---|---|
| She buys food at the grocery store. <br> She does not buy food at the grocery store. <br> She doesn't buy food at the grocery store. | 彼女は食料品店で食べ物を買います。 <br> 彼女は食料品店で食べ物を買いません。 |
| He gets stamps at the post office. <br> He does not get stamps at the post office. <br> He doesn't get stamps at the post office. | 彼は郵便局で切手を買います。 <br> 彼は郵便局で切手を買いません。 |

be 動詞の否定文を作るには not を付けるだけでよかったのを覚えていますか。そして be 動詞の否定文では代名詞と be の組み合わせを短縮したり (you + are = you're; she + is = she's)、be と not の組み合わせを短縮したりできます (are + not = aren't; is + not = isn't)。

| | |
|---|---|
| You're at the post office.<br>You're not at the post office.<br>You aren't at the post office. | あなたは郵便局にいます。<br>あなたは郵便局にいません。 |
| She's at the grocery store.<br>She's not at the grocery store.<br>She isn't at the grocery store. | 彼女は食料品店にいます。<br>彼女は食料品店にいません。 |

主語が I の場合、否定形の短縮方法は一種類しかありません。

| | |
|---|---|
| I'm at the office.<br>I'm not at the office. | 私は会社にいます。<br>私は会社にいません。 |

be 動詞を使った疑問文を作るには主語と動詞の順番を逆にします。

| | |
|---|---|
| New York is a big city.<br>Is New York a big city? | ニューヨークは大きな都市です。<br>ニューヨークは大きな都市ですか。 |
| Bill is at his office.<br>Is Bill at his office? | ビルさんは会社にいます。<br>ビルさんは会社にいますか。 |

be 動詞以外の動詞で疑問文を作るには do か does を使わなければなりません。

| | |
|---|---|
| They have dinner at seven o'clock.<br>Do they have dinner at seven o'clock? | 彼らは7時に夕飯を食べます。<br>彼らは7時に夕飯を食べますか。 |
| You work at a bank.<br>Do you work at a bank? | あなたは銀行で働きます。<br>あなたは銀行で働きますか。 |
| She lives in a small town.<br>Does she live in a small town? | 彼女は小さい町に住んでいます。<br>彼女は小さい町に住んでいますか。 |

Hello! How Are You?　　　Big or Small? Short or Tall?　　　Everyday Life

This Is My Family　　　Welcome to My Home

| He goes to work by train. | 彼は電車で仕事に行きます。 |
| Does he go to work by train? | 彼は電車で仕事に行きますか。 |

動詞 do を本動詞の「する」という意味で使って色々な事柄を言い表すことができます。

| The children do their homework after dinner. | 子供達は夕飯の後で宿題をします。 |
| We do the dishes after we eat. | 私達は食べた後で皿を洗います。 |
| Sarah is a good student; she does well at school. | サラさんは良い学生です。彼女は学校でよくできます。 |
| Max isn't a good student; he doesn't do well at school. | マックスさんは良い学生ではありません。彼は学校でよくできません。 |

## Vocabulary Builder 2

▶ 6D Vocabulary Builder 2 (CD 2, Track 14)

| New York is a very big city. | ニューヨークはとても大きな都市です。 |
| There are many tall buildings in New York. | ニューヨークには多くの高層ビルがあります。 |
| The Empire State Building is a famous building. | エンパイアステートビルは有名な建物です。 |
| It is at the intersection of Fifth Avenue and Thirty-Fourth Street. | それは五番街と34丁目の交差点にあります。 |
| There are very many streets with a lot of taxis, cars, and buses. | たくさんのタクシーや車やバスが通るとても多くの道があります。 |
| People in New York live in apartments. | ニューヨークの人々はアパートに住んでいます。 |
| They buy food in supermarkets or food stores. | 彼らはスーパーか食料品店で食べ物を買います。 |

**Essential English**

| People shop for clothes and other things at department stores. | 人々はデパートで洋服やその他の物を買います。 |
| Macy's and Bloomingdale's are famous department stores. | メーシーズとブルーミングデールズは有名なデパートです。 |
| People get bread at bakeries. | 人々はパン屋でパンを買います。 |
| They get meat at butcher shops. | 彼らは肉屋で肉を買います。 |
| There are many schools and universities in New York, too. | ニューヨークにはたくさんの学校や大学もあります。 |
| Many people work in office buildings. | たくさんの人々がオフィスビルで働きます。 |
| They get to work by subway, by bus, by taxi, or on foot. | 彼らは地下鉄かバスかタクシーか徒歩で仕事に行きます。 |
| There are big libraries with many books and computers. | たくさんの本とパソコンがある大きな図書館があります。 |
| There are many churches, synagogues, and mosques in New York. | ニューヨークにはたくさんの教会、シナゴーグ、それからモスクがあります。 |
| On weekends, many New Yorkers go to parks and relax. | 週末は多くのニューヨーカーは公園に行ってリラックスします。 |
| They also go to restaurants or to the movies. | 彼らはレストランや映画にも行きます。 |

## ✎ Vocabulary Practice 2

新出単語の練習です。空欄を埋めてください。ヒントが必要な場合はもう一度音声を聞いてみましょう。

1. New York is a very big _____.

2. There are many tall _____ in New York.

Hello! How Are You?　　　Big or Small? Short or Tall?　　　Everyday Life

This Is My Family　　　Welcome to My Home

3. The Empire State Building is a _____ building.

4. It is at the _____ of Fifth Avenue and Thirty-
   Fourth Street.

5. There are very many _____ with a lot of taxis, cars, and buses.

6. People in New York live in _____.

7. They buy food in _____ or food stores.

8. People shop for clothes and other things at _____
   stores.

9. Macy's and Bloomingdale's are _____ department stores.

10. People get bread at _____.

11. They get meat at _____ shops.

12. There are many _____ and universities in New York, too.

13. Many people work in _____ buildings.

14. They _____ to work by subway, by bus, by taxi, or on foot.

15. There are big _____ with many books and computers.

16. There are many _____, synagogues, and mosques in New
    York.

17. On weekends, many New Yorkers go to _____ and relax.

18. They also go to restaurants or to the _____.

答え
1. city; 2. buildings; 3. famous; 4. intersection; 5. streets; 6. apartments; 7. supermarkets; 8.
department; 9. famous; 10. bakeries; 11. butcher; 12. schools; 13. office; 14. get; 15. libraries;
16. churches; 17. parks; 18. movies

**Essential English**

## Grammar Builder 2

▶ 6E Grammar Builder 2 (CD 2, Track 15)

### 疑問文と疑問詞

**Be** 動詞を使って **yes/no** で答えられる疑問文を作ることはもうできますね。

| The children are at the park. | 子供達は公園にいます。 |
| Are the children at the park? | 子供達は公園にいますか。 |
| Mrs. Ramirez is a great professor. | ラミレズさんはとてもいい先生です。 |
| Is Mrs. Ramirez a great professor? | ラミレズさんはとてもいい先生ですか。 |

**have** などそれ以外の動詞を使って **yes/no** で答えられる疑問文を作るには **do** か **does** を用います。主語が **he/she/it** の時は **does** を使う代わりに、本動詞には **–(e)s** が付かないということを覚えておきましょう。

| They have a big family. | 彼らの家族は大家族です。 |
| Do they have a big family? | 彼らの家族は大家族ですか。 |
| John has a new computer. | ジョンさんは新しいパソコンを持っています。 |
| Does John have a new computer? | ジョンさんは新しいパソコンを持っていますか。 |
| Susan works in the city. | スーザンさんは市内で働いています。 |
| Does Susan work in the city? | スーザンさんは市内で働いていますか。 |

疑問詞を使って疑問文を作ることもできます。

| What? | 何？ |
| What does John do in the morning? | ジョンさんは朝に何をしますか。 |
| He eats breakfast in the morning. | 彼は朝に朝ご飯を食べます。 |
| Who? | 誰？ |
| Who do the students see in class? | 授業で学生は誰に会いますか。 |
| They see their professor in class. | 彼らは授業で先生に会います。 |

Hello! How Are You?          Big or Small? Short or Tall?          Everyday Life

This Is My Family                    Welcome to My Home

| | |
|---|---|
| When? | いつ？ |
| When does the train leave?<br>The train leaves at 9:05 in the morning. | いつ電車は発車しますか。<br>電車は午前9時5分に発車します。 |
| Where? | どこ？ |
| Where do Bill and Cynthia live?<br>They live in Chicago. | ビルさんとシンシアさんはどこに住んでいますか。<br>彼らはシカゴに住んでいます。 |
| How? | どうやって？ |
| How do you get to work?<br>I get to work by bus. | あなたはどうやって仕事に行きますか。<br>私はバスで仕事に行きます。 |
| Why? | どうして？ |
| Why do you buy bread at the bakery?<br>I buy bread at the bakery because it is good. | どうしてパン屋でパンを買うのですか。<br>おいしいからパン屋でパンを買います。 |

# ✎ Work Out 1

▶ 6F Work Out 1 (CD 2, Track 16)

音声を聞いて空欄を埋めてください。

1. _____ does Maria work?

2. She _____ at the university.

3. _____ does she do?

4. She _____ Spanish.

5. _____ does she have class?

6. She _____ class at one o'clock in the afternoon.

7. _____ does she teach?

8. She teaches _____.

9. _____ does she get to work?

10. She gets to work _____.

### 答え

1. Where; 2. works; 3. What; 4. teaches; 5. When; 6 has; 7. Who; 8. students; 9. How; 10. by car

## 🎙 Bring It All Together

▶ 6G Bring It All Together (CD 2, Track 17)

ミラさんとヘクターさんはスペイン語の授業をとっています。ミラさんがヘクターさんの住んでいる町のことについて尋ねています。聞いてみましょう。

| | |
|---|---|
| Mira: | Do you live in a big city or a small town, Hector? |
| ミラ： | ヘクターは大都市に住んでるの？それとも小さな町に住んでるの？ |
| Hector: | I live in a town. It's not small, but it's not very big. |
| ヘクター： | 僕は町に住んでるよ。小さくはないけど、すごく大きいわけでもないね。 |
| Mira: | Is it far from the university? |
| ミラ： | 大学から遠い？ |
| Hector: | Yes, it's in New York. |
| ヘクター： | うん、ニューヨークなんだ。 |
| Mira: | But New York is a big city! |
| ミラ： | でもニューヨークは大都市じゃない！ |
| Hector: | New York is also a state. I live in a town in New York state. |
| ヘクター： | ニューヨークは州の名前でもあるんだ。僕はニューヨーク州の町に住んでるんだよ。 |
| Mira: | Oh, right. Is your town near New York City? |
| ミラ： | ああそうか。あなたの町はニューヨーク市の近く？ |

だいいっか 6: Around Town    113

Hello! How Are You?          Big or Small? Short or Tall?          Everyday Life

This Is My Family          Welcome to My Home

| | |
|---|---|
| Hector: | It's about two hours away from the city. There are trains and buses that go to the city. My father works in the city. He takes the train to the city very early every morning. |
| ヘクター： | 市から2時間ぐらいのところだね。市内まで行く電車やバスがあるよ。父は市で働いているんだ。毎朝とても早く電車に乗って市まで行ってるよ。 |
| Mira: | Who do you live with? |
| ミラ： | ヘクターは誰と住んでいるの？ |
| Hector: | I live with my mother and father, and I have two sisters. |
| ヘクター： | 母と父と住んでいて、それから二人の姉（妹）がいるよ。 |
| Mira: | Are there a lot of stores in your town? |
| ミラ： | 町にはたくさんお店がある？ |
| Hector: | Yes, there's a supermarket, clothing stores, a bakery, a butcher shop, a department store, and three or four convenience stores. |
| ヘクター： | うん、スーパーと洋服屋とパン屋と肉屋とデパートと三、四件コンビニがあるよ。 |
| Mira: | Do you live in the center of town? |
| ミラ： | 町の中心部に住んでいるの？ |
| Hector: | No, there aren't many houses in the center of town. There are a lot of stores, restaurants, a few banks, a park, the school, the post office, some churches, and a few apartment buildings, but not many houses. |
| ヘクター： | いや、町の中心部にはあまり家がないんだ。たくさんの店やレストラン、銀行が数軒、公園、学校、郵便局、教会が何軒か、それからアパートが数軒あるけど、家はあまりないんだ。 |
| Mira: | Do you go home often? |
| ミラ： | 家にはよく帰るの？ |
| Hector: | I go home and see my family once or twice each semester. |
| ヘクター： | 毎学期、一、二度家へ帰って家族に会うよ。 |
| Mira: | How do you get home? |
| ミラ： | どうやって家に帰るの？ |

| Hector: | I go home by train usually. |
| ヘクター： | 大抵電車で帰るね。 |
| Mira: | And what do you do? |
| ミラ： | それで、何をするの？ |
| Hector: | I relax, I spend time with my family, and I see my friends. |
| ヘクター： | リラックスしたり家族と過ごしたり、友達に会ったりするんだ。 |
| Mira: | That's nice. I come from Croatia, so I don't go home very often. |
| ミラ： | それはいいわね。私はクロアチア出身だから実家にはそんなにしょっちゅうは帰らないわ。 |
| Hector: | And where in Croatia do you come from? |
| ヘクター： | クロアチアのどこ出身？ |
| Mira: | I come from Zagreb. |
| ミラ： | ザグレブよ。 |
| Hector: | Is that a small town? |
| ヘクター： | それは小さい町？ |
| Mira: | No, it's a city. It's the capital of the country. |
| ミラ： | いいえ、都市よ。クロアチアの首都なの。 |
| Hector: | And why are you studying Spanish? |
| ヘクター： | それでどうしてスペイン語を勉強してるの？ |
| Mira: | I'm studying Spanish because I like the language a lot, and because many people speak Spanish. It's a useful language. And why are you studying Spanish? Isn't Hector a Spanish name? |
| ミラ： | スペイン語がとても好きだし、たくさんの人が話すからスペイン語を勉強してるの。役に立つ言葉だわ。どうしてヘクターはスペイン語を勉強してるの？ヘクターってスペイン語の名前じゃない？ |
| Hector: | Yes, Hector is a Spanish name. My family is originally from Mexico. |
| ヘクター： | うん、ヘクターはスペイン語の名前だよ。僕の家族はもともとメキシコから来たんだ。 |
| Mira: | You don't speak Spanish already? |
| ミラ： | もうスペイン語を話せるんじゃないの？ |

Hello! How Are You?          Big or Small? Short or Tall?          Everyday Life

This Is My Family          Welcome to My Home

| | |
|---|---|
| Hector: | No, I don't. My sisters and I only speak English. My parents speak English and Spanish, and my grandparents only speak Spanish. |
| ヘクター: | いや、話せないんだ。姉（妹）と僕は英語しか話さないんだよ。両親は英語とスペイン語を話して、祖父母はスペイン語しか話さないよ。 |
| Mira: | So you're studying Spanish because your family is from Mexico? |
| ミラ: | じゃあ、ご家族がメキシコから来たからスペイン語を勉強してるの？ |
| Hector: | Yes, that's right. And also because it's a useful second language in the United States. |
| ヘクター: | うん、そうだよ。それからアメリカでは役に立つ第二言語だからだね。 |

## Take It Further

▶ 6H Take It Further (CD 2, Track 18)

会話の中でヘクターさんがミラさんに以下の質問をしました。

| Why are you studying Spanish? | どうしてスペイン語を勉強してるの？ |
|---|---|

単純現在形はもう既に知っていますね。

| I study Spanish at the university. | 私は大学でスペイン語を勉強します。 |
|---|---|
| We eat dinner at seven in the evening. | 私達は夜7時に夕飯を食べます。 |

日常的に繰り返される行動について話す時は単純現在形を使います。単純現在形は **generally** (だいたい), **usually** (たいてい), **always** (いつも), **on Monday** (月曜日に), **every day** (毎日), **at seven o'clock** (7時に) などの表現と一緒によく使われます。

| Hector's grandparents always speak Spanish. | ヘクターさんの祖父母はいつもスペイン語を話します。 |
|---|---|
| Hector's mother speaks English with her children, but she speaks Spanish with her parents. | ヘクターさんのお母さんはお子さんとは英語を話しますが、彼女はご両親とはスペイン語を話します。 |

| Hector studies Spanish every Monday, Wednesday, and Friday. | ヘクターさんは毎週月曜日と水曜日と金曜日にスペイン語を勉強します。 |
| Hector usually sees his family once or twice each semester. | ヘクターさんはたいてい毎学期一、二度家族に会います。 |

現在進行形 be + ing を使うと、今起こっていることを表現することができます。

| You are studying English right now. | あなたは今英語を勉強しています。 |
| You are reading a sentence in English. | あなたは英文を読んでいます。 |
| Mira is in Croatia now, so she's speaking Croatian. (But she also speaks English.) | ミラさんは今クロアチアにいますから、クロアチア語を話しています。(でも、彼女は英語も話します。) |
| Hector's mother is with her children now, so she's speaking English. (But she also speaks Spanish.) | ヘクターさんのお母さんは今お子さんと一緒にいますので、英語を話しています。(でも彼女はスペイン語も話します。) |

現在進行形についてはもう少し後で詳しく勉強します。

---

## ✎ Work Out 2
各文を否定文に直してください。

例: **I work in a bank.**
答え: **I do not/don't work in a bank.**

1. **She goes to work by train.**

   _____

2. **The professor teaches every Wednesday.**

   _____

Hello! How Are You?          Big or Small? Short or Tall?          Everyday Life

This Is My Family          Welcome to My Home

3. We eat at the restaurant every Friday.

   _____

4. I get gas at the gas station in the morning.

   _____

5. John buys bread at the bakery.

   _____

6. She buys milk at the convenience store.

   _____

7. They get stamps at the post office.

   _____

8. Bill is at the bank.

   _____

**答え**

1. She does not go/doesn't go to work by train. 2. The professor does not teach/doesn't teach every Wednesday. 3. We do not eat/don't eat at the restaurant every Friday. 4. I do not get/don't get gas at the gas station in the morning. 5. John does not buy/doesn't buy bread at the bakery. 6. She does not buy/doesn't buy milk at the convenience store. 7. They do not get/don't get stamps at the post office. 8. Bill is not/isn't at the bank.

今度は疑問文を作ってください。

例: Bill works <u>at a clothing store</u>.
答え: Where does Bill work?

1. Mira studies <u>Spanish</u> at the university. _____

2. Hector sees <u>his friends</u> at home. _____

3. The train leaves <u>at 9:05 a.m.</u> _____

4. Hector's father goes to work in the city <u>by train.</u>

_____

5. Jasmine lives <u>in a small town.</u> _____

6. They buy milk at the convenience store <u>because it's near their apartment.</u>

_____

**答え**
1. What does Mira study at the university? 2. Who does Hector see at home? 3. When does the train leave? (または What time does the train leave?) 4. How does Hector's father go to work in the city? 5. Where does Jasmine live? 6. Why do they buy milk at the convenience store?

## ✎ Drive It Home

それぞれの文を否定文、yes/no で答えられる疑問文、そして疑問詞を使った疑問文にしてください。

例: Hank works at a gas station.
答え: Hank doesn't work at a gas station.
Does Hank work at a gas station?
Where does Hank work?

1. Bob and Mary live <u>in a big house.</u> _____

2. They buy <u>their food</u> at the supermarket. _____

3. The students see <u>their professor</u> every morning.

_____

4. Gloria leaves work <u>at 5:45.</u>_____

5. Joe goes to work <u>by bus.</u>_____

Hello! How Are You?    Big or Small? Short or Tall?    Everyday Life

This Is My Family    Welcome to My Home

6. You eat at the restaurant <u>because the food is good.</u>

_____

**答え**
1. Bob and Mary don't live in a big house. Do Bob and Mary live in a big house? Where do Bob and Mary live? 2. They don't buy their food at the supermarket. Do they buy their food at the supermarket? What do they buy at the supermarket? 3. The students don't see their professor every morning. Do the students see their professor every morning? Who do the students see every morning? 4. Gloria doesn't leave work at 5:45. Does Gloria leave work at 5:45? When (What time) does Gloria leave work? 5. Joe doesn't go to work by bus. Does Joe go to work by bus? How does Joe go to work? 6. You don't eat at the restaurant because the food is good. Do you eat at the restaurant because the food is good? Why do you eat at the restaurant?

## Parting Words

**Well done!** (よくできました!)これで第6課は終了です。学習した内容を確認してみましょう。

☐ **town** や **city** にある色々な場所に関する基礎的な語彙 (まだ自信がない場合は p.103 に戻って復習しましょう。)

☐ **do** と **does** を含む疑問文と否定文 (まだ自信がない場合は p.106 に戻って復習しましょう。)

☐ 場所に関する更なる語彙 (まだ自信がない場合は p.108 に戻って復習しましょう。)

☐ 疑問詞 (まだ自信がない場合は p.111 に戻って復習しましょう。)

☐ 学習した項目を使って会話をする (まだ自信がない場合は p.113 に戻って復習しましょう。)

www.livinglanguage.com/languagelab のページをチェックするのを忘れずに。バーチャル単語帳やゲームやクイズで、学習したことを復習してみましょう!

# Word Recall

適切な単語を空欄に埋めてください。

1. People get money at the _____.

2. People buy _____ and mail _____ at the post office.

3. People buy food at the _____ store or

   _____ .

4. People buy clothes at the _____ store.

5. People eat at the _____ .

6. People get gas at the _____ .

7. People buy coffee, newspapers, and magazines at the

   _____ store.

8. There are tall _____ in cities.

9. The Empire State Building is at the _____ of Fifth

   Avenue and Thirty-Fourth Street.

10. There are cars, taxis, and buses on the _____ .

11. People in cities often live in _____ , not houses.

12. People shop for clothes and other things at _____

    stores.

13. People get bread at the _____ .

14. People get meat at the _____ shop.

15. In cities, many people work in _____ buildings.

16. People in cities get to work by _____, by bus, by taxi, or on foot.

17. There are many books and computers in _____.

18. In cities, many people go to _____ to walk or relax.

答え
1. bank または ATM; 2. stamps, letters; 3. grocery または food, supermarket; 4. Clothing/
department または 5. restaurant; 6. gas station; 7. convenience; 8. buildings; 9. intersection;
10. street/streets; 11. apartments; 12. department; 13. bakery; 14. butcher; 15. office; 16.
subway/train; 17. libraries; 18. parks

# だいいっか 7: いただきます!

## Lesson 7: Let's Eat!

本課ではレストランに行きますよ。レッスン内容は以下の通りです。

- ☐ 食事やレストランに関する語彙
- ☐ 丁寧なお願いの仕方
- ☐ 食べ物に関する語彙
- ☐ some と any の使い方
- ☐ 学習した項目を使ってレストランで食事を注文する
  それでは始めましょう。Enjoy the meal! (食事を楽しんで!)

Hello! How Are You?　　　Big or Small? Short or Tall?　　　Everyday Life

This Is My Family　　　　　Welcome to My Home

# Vocabulary Builder 1

▶ 7A Vocabulary Builder 1 (CD 2, Track 19)

| People eat breakfast in the morning. | 人々は朝、朝食を食べます。 |
|---|---|
| People often eat eggs, toast, or cereal for breakfast. | 人々は朝食によく卵やトーストやシリアルを食べます。 |
| People eat lunch around noon. | 人々は昼の12時頃に昼ご飯を食べます。 |
| People often eat sandwiches for lunch. | 人々は昼ご飯によくサンドイッチを食べます。 |
| People eat dinner in the evening. | 人々は夜に夕飯を食べます。 |
| Dinner is usually a big meal. | 夕飯はたいてい量の多い食事です。 |
| People eat with a fork, knife, and spoon. | 人々はフォークとナイフとスプーンを使って食べます。 |
| The food is on a plate, and the drink is in a glass. | 食べ物はお皿の上に載っていて、飲み物はコップに入っています。 |
| Before the meal at a restaurant, the server gives customers the menu. | レストランでは食事の前にウェイターが客にメニューを渡します。 |
| People first choose an appetizer. | 人々は最初に前菜を選びます。 |
| Appetizers are usually salads or small dishes. | 前菜はたいていサラダか小皿に盛られた料理です。 |
| After the appetizer, the server brings the main course. | 前菜の後で、ウェイターはメインディッシュを持ってきます。 |
| The main course is usually meat, pasta, or vegetables. | メインディッシュはたいてい肉かパスタか野菜です。 |
| After the main course, some people eat dessert. | メインディッシュの後でデザートを食べる人もいます。 |
| Dessert is usually cake, pie, or ice cream. | デザートはたいていケーキかパイかアイスクリームです。 |

| People often drink coffee or tea with dessert. | 人々はよくデザートと一緒にコーヒーか紅茶を飲みます。 |
| After the meal, the server brings the bill. | 食事の後でウェイターはお勘定を持ってきます。 |

# Take it Further

▶ 7B Take It Further (CD 2, Track 20)

「食べる」と言うには動詞 eat か have を使います。

| People eat breakfast in the morning. People have breakfast in the morning. | 人々は朝、朝食を食べます。 |
| People eat lunch around noon. People have lunch around noon. | 人々は昼の12時頃に昼ご飯を食べます。 |
| People eat dinner in the evening. People have dinner in the evening. | 人々は夜に夕飯を食べます。 |

dinner の代わりに supper と言うこともできます。

| What time do you usually have supper? | たいてい何時に夕飯を食べますか。 |

appetizer の代わりに starter と言うこともできます。

| Are you having a starter before the main course? | メインディッシュの前に前菜を食べますか。 |

bill の代わりに check と言うこともできます。

| At the end of a meal, the customer says "check, please!" or "could we please have the bill?" | 食事の後で、客は「お勘定をお願いします!」あるいは「お勘定をお願いできますか」と言います。 |

Hello! How Are You?          Big or Small? Short or Tall?          Everyday Life

This Is My Family                    Welcome to My Home

server は男性にも女性にも使える単語ですが、waiter は男性のみ、waitress は女性のみに使われます。

| The waiter brings us the menu. | ウェイターはメニューを持ってきます。 |
| We ask the waitress for the check. | 私達はウェイトレスにお勘定をお願いします。 |

# ✎ Vocabulary Practice 1

適切な単語で空欄を埋めてください。

1. People eat _____ in the morning.

2. People often eat eggs, toast, or _____ for breakfast.

3. People eat _____ around noon.

4. People often eat _____ for lunch.

5. People eat _____ in the evening.

6. Dinner is usually a big _____.

7. People eat with a _____, _____ and spoon, and drink from a

   _____.

8. Before the meal at a restaurant, the server gives customers the

   _____.

9. People first choose an _____.

10. Appetizers are usually salads or small _____.

11. After the appetizer, the server brings the _____ course.

12. The main course is usually _____, pasta, or vegetables.

13. **After the main course, some people eat** _____.

14. **Dessert is usually** _____, **pie, or ice cream.**

15. **People often drink coffee or** _____ **with dessert.**

16. **After the meal, the server brings the** _____.

**答え**

1. breakfast; 2. cereal; 3. lunch; 4. sandwiches; 5. dinner/supper; 6. meal; 7. fork, knife, glass; 8. menu; 9. appetizer; 10. dishes; 11. main; 12. meat; 13. dessert; 14. cake; 15. tea; 16. bill/ check

## 🌐 Culture Note

アメリカ人は **to eat out** (外食すること) が大好きです。様々な **cuisines** (〜料理) を楽しみます。たとえば、フランス料理、イタリア料理、中華料理、スペイン料理、メキシコ料理、日本料理、韓国料理などをはじめとして様々な地域の料理を楽しみます。レストランではウェイターに **tip** (チップ)を置きます。とても良いサービスを受けた場合のチップはたいてい勘定の20% です。サービスがまあまあだった場合は15%です。そして、友人同士で外食する場合はたいてい勘定を **split** します。勘定を分けるということです。これは **going Dutch** (割り勘)と呼ばれることもあります。

## Grammar Builder 1

▶ 7C Grammar Builder 1 (CD 2, Track 21)

### お願いの仕方

命令文を言うには、動詞を –(e)s の語尾無しでそのまま使えばいいのですが、**please** を添えることによって丁寧なお願いになります。

| | |
|---|---|
| **Please bring the menu.** | メニューを持ってきてください。 |
| **Please bring more bread.** | もっとパンを持ってきてください。 |
| **Pass the milk, please.** | ミルクをとってください。 |

Hello! How Are You?　　　Big or Small? Short or Tall?　　　Everyday Life

This Is My Family　　　Welcome to My Home

もっと丁寧にお願いをしたい場合は could you please ...?を使ってみましょう。

| Could you please bring the menu? | メニューを持ってきていただけますか。 |
| Could you please pass the salt? | 塩をとっていただけますか。 |
| Could you please bring the check? | お勘定を持ってきていただけますか。 |

would like も丁寧な表現です。

| I would like the menu, please. | メニューをいただきたいのですが。 |
| We would like a table for two. | 二名でテーブルをお願いしたいのですが。 |
| Would you like dessert? | デザートはいかがですか。 |

# Vocabulary Builder 2

▶ 7D Vocabulary Builder 2 (CD 2, Track 22)

| Beef, pork, and lamb are kinds of meat. | 牛肉と豚肉とラムは肉の種類です。 |
| Chicken, duck, and turkey are kinds of poultry. | 鶏肉と鴨と七面鳥は鳥肉の種類です。 |
| Carrots, lettuce, cucumbers, and spinach are vegetables. | にんじんとレタスときゅうりとほうれん草は野菜です。 |
| Oranges, apples, bananas, and pears are kinds of fruit. | オレンジとリンゴとバナナと洋梨は果物の種類です。 |
| People often eat bread with butter on it. | 人々はよくパンにバターを塗って食べます。 |
| Italy is famous for pasta dishes, for example, spaghetti with tomato sauce. | イタリアはパスタ料理が有名です。パスタ料理の例はトマトソースのスパゲッティです。 |
| France is famous for cheese and wine. | フランスはチーズとワインが有名です。 |

| Germany is famous for beer. | ドイツはビールが有名です。 |
| People in Japan, China, and Korea eat a lot of rice. | 日本と中国と韓国の人々はたくさん米を食べます。 |
| There is rice and raw fish in sushi. | おすしは米と生魚でできています。 |
| Hamburgers, hot dogs, and fries are American fast food. | ハンバーガーとホットドッグとフライドポテトはアメリカのファーストフードです。 |
| Many people drink orange juice, coffee, or tea at breakfast. | 多くの人は朝食時にオレンジジュースやコーヒーや紅茶を飲みます。 |

# ✎ Vocabulary Practice 2

新出ボキャブラリーの練習です。

1. What are three examples of meat? _____

2. What are three kinds of poultry? _____

3. Give four examples of vegetables. _____

4. What are four kinds of fruit? _____

5. What do people often put on their bread? _____

6. Spaghetti often comes with what kind of sauce? _____

7. What two things is France famous for? _____

8. What kind of drink is Germany famous for? _____

9. What kind of food do people in Japan, China, and Korea often eat? _____

10. What is there in sushi? _____

11. What are three common American fast foods? _____

12. What are three common breakfast drinks? _____

Hello! How Are You?          Big or Small? Short or Tall?          Everyday Life

This Is My Family                    Welcome to My Home

**答え**
1. beef, pork, and lamb; 2. chicken, duck, and turkey; 3. carrots, lettuce, cucumbers, and
spinach; 4. oranges, apples, bananas, and pears; 5. butter; 6. tomato; 7. wine and cheese; 8.
beer; 9. rice; 10. rice and raw fish; 11. hamburgers, hot dogs, and fries; 12. orange juice,
coffee, and tea.

# Grammar Builder 2
▶ 7E Grammar Builder 2 (CD 2, Track 23)

## SOME と ANY

不特定の量を表すには名詞の前に some をつけます。

| Please bring me some water. | お水を持ってきてください。 |
| We would like some bread. | パンをいただきたいのですが。 |
| I would like some milk and sugar in my coffee. | コーヒーにミルクと砂糖が欲しいのですが。 |

数えられる名詞 (one person, two people; one student, two students) の前に
some を使う時は名詞を複数形にします。

| Some people drink red wine, and some people drink white wine. | 赤ワインを飲む人もいれば、白ワインを飲む人もいます。 |
| There are some tables near the window. | 窓のそばにテーブルがいくつかあります。 |
| Some students in the class are excellent, but some are not very good. | このクラスには優秀な学生もいれば、あまり良くない学生もいます。 |

Some は疑問文の中で不特定の量を表すのにも使われます。

| Would you like some vegetables? | 野菜はいかがですか。 |
| Do you have some money for me? | 私に貸せるお金がいくらかありますか。 |

Around Town | Let's Go Shopping | What Do You Feel Like Doing?

Let's Eat! | At Work

**Any** は否定文で使用します。

| | |
|---|---|
| I have <u>some</u> bread. | 私はパンがあります。 |
| I don't have <u>any</u> bread. | 私はパンがありません。 |
| There are <u>some</u> excellent restaurants in this town. | この町には（いくつかの）とても良いレストランがあります。 |
| There aren't <u>any</u> excellent restaurants in this town. | この町にはとても良いレストランは一つもありません。 |
| I have <u>some</u> friends from Germany. | 私はドイツ出身の友達が（何人か）います。 |
| I don't have <u>any</u> friends from Germany. | 私はドイツ出身の友達が一人もいません。 |

**Any** は疑問文でも使われます。

| | |
|---|---|
| Would you like any vegetables? | 何か野菜は好きですか。 |
| Do you have any brothers or sisters? | ご兄弟はいますか。 |
| Does she have any good books? | 彼女は何かいい本を持っていますか。 |

# ✎ Work Out 1

▶ 7F Work Out 1 (CD 2, Track 24)

音声を聞いて空欄を埋めてください。

1. We _____ like a table for two.

2. Are there _____ tables next to the window?

3. _____ you please bring the menu?

4. We don't have _____ forks on the table.

5. We would like _____ bread, please.

6. Pass the salt, _____ .

Hello! How Are You?     Big or Small? Short or Tall?     Everyday Life

This Is My Family     Welcome to My Home

7. Please bring _____ water.

8. Would you like _____ butter?

9. We would like _____ dessert.

10. Could you please _____ the bill?

**答え**
1. would; 2. any; 3. Could; 4. any; 5. some; 6. please; 7. some; 8. any; 9. some; 10. bring

# Bring It All Together

▶ 7G Bring It All Together (CD 2, Track 25)

ジョンさんとポーラさんは町に新しくできたイタリアンレストラン *Cucina*(クチーナ)に来ています。注文をしようとしているようです。聞いてみましょう。

| | |
|---|---|
| Waiter: | Good evening, and welcome to Cucina. Would you like the wine list? |
| ウェイター: | こんばんは、クチーナへようこそ。ワインリストはご覧になりますか。 |
| Paula: | Hmmm ... No, I don't want any wine, thank you. But I would like some water, please. |
| ポーラ: | えっと・・・いいえ、ワインはいりません。ありがとうございます。お水をいただきたいのですが。 |
| John: | Water is good for me, too. |
| ジョン: | 私もお水で結構です。 |
| Waiter: | Certainly. Would you like an appetizer? |
| ウェイター: | かしこまりました。前菜はいかがですか。 |
| Paula: | What do you think, John, the bruschetta? |
| ポーラ: | ジョン、ブルスケッタはどうかしら? |
| John: | Yes, that sounds good. And maybe the fresh mozzarella plate. |
| ジョン: | うん、いいね。それから新鮮なモッツァレラチーズもいいかな。 |
| Waiter: | Okay, I'll be right back with some water and your appetizers. |
| ウェイター: | はい、それではお水と前菜をすぐにお持ちいたします。 |
| Paula: | So, what are you having? |

| ポーラ: | ジョンは何を頼むの？ |
|---|---|
| John: | The roast chicken looks good. But the shrimp looks good, too. I'm not sure. |
| ジョン: | ローストチキンがおいしそうだなあ。でも海老もおいしそうだし。まだ分からないよ。 |
| Paula: | I'd like pasta tonight. The lasagna looks good, but we're having mozzarella as an appetizer. |
| ポーラ: | 今夜はパスタが食べたいわ。ラザーニャがおいしそうだけど、前菜でモッツァレラチーズをいただくのよね。 |
| John: | Yeah, maybe that's too much cheese. How about the spaghetti with the tomato and basil sauce? |
| ジョン: | うん、ちょっとチーズの量が多すぎちゃうね。トマトとバジルのソースのスパゲッティはどう？ |
| Paula: | Yes, that sounds good. Oh, here's our waiter. |
| ポーラ: | ええ、それはおいしそうだわ。あ、ウェイターが来たわよ。 |
| Waiter: | So, here are your starters, and two glasses of water. What would you like as a main course? Ma'am? |
| ウェイター: | こちらが前菜になりまして、こちらがお水です。[ポーラさんに] メインのお料理は何になさいますか。 |
| Paula: | I would like the spaghetti with tomato and basil. |
| ポーラ: | トマトとバジルのスパゲッティをお願いします。 |
| Waiter: | Perfect. And for you, sir? |
| ウェイター: | かしこまりました。[ジョンさんに] 何になさいますか。 |
| John: | I would like the baked shrimp. |
| ジョン: | ベイクドシュリンプをお願いします。 |
| Waiter: | Okay. And would you like any vegetables with that? Tonight we have baked potatoes, sautéed spinach, or grilled eggplant. |
| ウェイター: | かしこまりました。添え物に野菜はいかがですか。今夜はベイクドポテトとほうれん草のソテーとなすのグリル焼きがございます。 |
| Paula: | Oh, I love eggplant. I'll have the grilled eggplant, please. |
| ポーラ: | 私はなすが大好きだわ。なすのグリル焼きをお願いします。 |
| John: | And I'll have the spinach. |

Hello! How Are You?          Big or Small? Short or Tall?          Everyday Life

This Is My Family                    Welcome to My Home

| | |
|---|---|
| ジョン: | 私はほうれん草をお願いします。 |
| **Waiter:** | **Okay, I'll bring those dishes in just a moment. Enjoy your appetizers!** |
| ウェイター: | かしこまりました。すぐにお料理をお持ちいたします。前菜をお楽しみください! |

## Take It Further

▶ 7H Take It Further (CD 2, Track 26)

会話の中に sounds good と looks good という表現が出てきましたね。何かを聞いて、それをいいなと思ったら sounds good といいます。

| The music sounds good! | この音楽はいいですね! |
|---|---|
| Mary sounds good when she sings. | メアリーさんは歌うのが上手です。 |
| How about some coffee?<br>Oh, yeah. That sounds good. | コーヒーはいかが? ええ、いいわね。 |

何かを見て、それをいいなと思ったら looks good といいます。

| The cake looks good! I want some. | このケーキはおいしそうですね!少しいただきたいです。 |
|---|---|
| There's a new restaurant, and the menu looks really good. | 新しいレストランがあるのですが、メニューを見た限りではとても良さそうです。 |
| Your photos of Paris look really good. | あなたのパリの写真はとてもいいです。 |

too much という表現も会話に出てきました。

| I want one glass of wine. That's two glasses of wine. That's too much wine! | ワインが一杯欲しいです。これはワイン二杯です。これは多すぎます! |
|---|---|
| Cheese for an appetizer and in the main course? That's too much cheese! | 前菜とメインディッシュでチーズ? それは多すぎですよ! |

Around Town | Let's Go Shopping | What Do You Feel Like Doing?

Let's Eat! | At Work

次のレッスンでは **too much, too many, little, a few** などの表現について詳しく見ていきます。

---

## ✎ Work Out 2

丁寧なお願いの仕方を練習しましょう。例にならって各文を丁寧な言い方に変えてください。

例: **Pass the milk, please.**
答え: **Could you please pass the milk?**

1. **Bring the menu, please.**

   _____

2. **Bring some bread, please.**

   _____

3. **Pass the salt, please.**

   _____

4. **Read the wine list, please.**

   _____

5. **Bring a fork and a knife, please.**

   _____

**答え**
1. Could you please bring the menu? 2. Could you please bring some bread? 3. Could you please pass the salt? 4. Could you please read the wine list? 5. Could you please bring a fork and a knife?

今度は **some** か **any** のうちで適切な方を 空欄に埋めてください。

Hello! How Are You?          Big or Small? Short or Tall?          Everyday Life

This Is My Family                    Welcome to My Home

1. I would like _____ sugar in my tea.

2. We would like _____ bread and butter.

3. We don't have _____ tables near the window.

4. There are _____ very good restaurants in this town.

5. Would you like _____ vegetables with your main courses?

6. Do you have _____ brothers or sisters?

7. I have _____ friends at the university.

8. There aren't _____ Thai restaurants near here.

9. I would like _____ coffee, please.

10. I don't want _____ dessert.

答え
1. some; 2. some; 3. any; 4. some; 5. any; 6. any; 7. some; 8. any; 9. some; 10. any

## ✎ Drive It Home

some を使って肯定文を、そして any を使って否定文と疑問文を作ってください。

例: There is … cheese in the pasta.
答え: There is some cheese in the pasta. There isn't any cheese in the pasta. Is there any cheese in the pasta?

1. She reads … books in French.

_____

2. There is … sugar in your tea.

_____

Around Town | Let's Go Shopping | What Do You Feel Like Doing?

Let's Eat!  At Work

3. They have … tables next to the windows.

_____

4. There is … meat in the dish.

_____

5. John has … friends from Canada.

_____

6. She sees … people in the library.

_____

**答え**

1. She reads some books in French. She doesn't read any books in French. Does she read any books in French? 2. There is some sugar in your tea. There isn't any sugar in your tea. Is there any sugar in your tea? 3. They have some tables next to the windows. They don't have any tables next to the windows. Do they have any tables next to the windows? 4. There is some meat in the dish. There isn't any meat in the dish. Is there any meat in the dish? 5. John has some friends from Canada. John doesn't have any friends from Canada. Does John have any friends from Canada? 6. She sees some people in the library. She doesn't see any people in the library. Does she see any people in the library?

## Parting Words

**Fantastic!**（すばらしいです！）これで第7課は終了です。学習した内容を確認しましょう。

☐ 食事やレストランに関する語彙　（まだ自信がない場合は p.124 に戻って復習しましょう。）

☐ 丁寧なお願いの仕方　（まだ自信がない場合は p.127 に戻って復習しましょう。）

☐ 食べ物に関する語彙　（まだ自信がない場合は p.128 に戻って復習しましょう。）

☐ some と any の使い方　（まだ自信がない場合は p.130 に戻って復習しましょう。）

Hello! How Are You?　　　Big or Small? Short or Tall?　　　Everyday Life

This Is My Family　　　Welcome to My Home

□ 学習した項目を使ってレストランで食事を注文する　（まだ自信がない場合は p.132 に戻って復習しましょう。）

www.livinglanguage.com/languagelab のページをチェックするのを忘れずに。バーチャル単語帳やゲームやクイズで、学習したことを復習してみましょう！

# Word Recall

第7課で出てきた単語を覚えているか確認してみましょう。

1. People eat _____ in the morning.

2. For breakfast, people often eat _____, toast, or cereal.

3. People eat _____ around noon.

4. For lunch, people often eat _____.

5. People eat _____ in the evening.

6. People use a _____, a _____, and a _____ to eat.

7. People drink from a _____.

8. At a restaurant, people first choose an _____.

9. Then, people choose the _____ course.

10. After the meal, people sometimes eat _____.

11. Beef, _____, and lamb are kinds of meat.

12. _____, duck, and turkey are kinds of poultry.

13. Carrots, lettuce, cucumbers, and spinach are _____.

14. Oranges, apples, bananas, and pears are kinds of _____.

15. People often eat bread with _____ on it.

**答え**
1. breakfast; 2. eggs; 3. lunch; 4. sandwiches; 5. dinner (または supper); 6. fork, knife, spoon; 7. glass (または cup); 8. appetizer; 9. main; 10. dessert; 11. pork; 12. Chicken; 13. vegetables; 14. fruit; 15. butter

Hello! How Are You?      Big or Small? Short or Tall?      Everyday Life

This Is My Family      Welcome to My Home

# だいいっか 8: 買い物に行きましょう。

## Lesson 8: Let's Go Shopping

**Welcome to Lesson 8!**（第8課へようこそ!）本課では買い物に行きますよ。レッスン内容は以下の通りです。

□ 店の名前や買い物に関する語彙

□ **many** や **much** といった数量を表す言葉

□ **clothing**（衣服）の種類

□ 比較級 (**bigger** など) と最上級 (**biggest** など)

□ 買い物に関する会話の中で学習した項目を総合的に使う
準備はいいですか?

Around Town      **Let's Go Shopping**      What Do You Feel Like Doing?

Let's Eat!      At Work

# Vocabulary Builder 1

▶ 8A Vocabulary Builder 1 (CD 2, Track 27)

| | |
|---|---|
| People go to stores to buy things. | 人々は店に行って物を買います。 |
| People usually pay with cash or by credit card. | 人々はたいてい現金かカードで支払います。 |
| Mary needs shoes, so she goes to the shoe store. | メアリーさんは靴が要るので靴屋に行きます。 |
| John wants a new book, so he goes to the bookstore. | ジョンさんは新しい本が欲しいので本屋に行きます。 |
| People buy food at grocery stores or at supermarkets. | 人々は食料品店かスーパーで食べ物を買います。 |
| Some people buy bread at a bakery. | パン屋でパンを買う人もいます。 |
| Some people buy meat at a butcher shop. | 肉屋で肉を買う人もいます。 |
| Electronics stores sell computers, televisions, and stereos. | 電器屋ではパソコンやテレビやステレオを売っています。 |
| Hardware stores sell paint, hammers, nails, and other things to fix the house. | 金物屋ではペンキやハンマーや釘やその他、家を修理する物を売っています。 |
| Department stores sell all kinds of things, especially clothes. | デパートでは色々な種類の物、特に洋服を売っています。 |
| Things are cheaper when they're on sale. | セールの時は物が安いです。 |
| There are a lot of different stores in a mall. | ショッピングモールには色々な店があります。 |
| Many people like to go shopping in malls. | 多くの人はショッピングモールで買い物をするのが好きです。 |
| They spend a lot of money, and a lot of time, in malls. | 彼らはショッピングモールでたくさんのお金と時間を費やします。 |

Hello! How Are You?          Big or Small? Short or Tall?          Everyday Life

This Is My Family          Welcome to My Home

## Take it Further

▶ 8B Take It Further (CD 2, Track 28)

spend という動詞が出てきましたね。私達は物に spend money、すなわちお金を費やします。

| Houses are expensive, so you spend a lot of money on a new house. | 家は高いです。なのであなたは新しい家にたくさんのお金を費やします。 |
|---|---|
| At Christmas, many people spend a lot of money on gifts. | クリスマスにはたくさんの人がプレゼントにたくさんのお金を費やします。 |
| We spend two hundred dollars a week on food. | 私達は一週間に食費に200ドルを費やします。 |

それから私達は物事に spend time、すなわち時間を費やしますね。

| Mary is a very good student. She spends three hours every night at the library. | メアリーさんはとても良い学生です。彼女は毎晩図書館で3時間過ごします。 |
|---|---|
| The kids spend too much time watching television! | 子供達はテレビを見る時間を費やしすぎます。 |
| We spend two weeks every year in Puerto Rico on vacation. | 私達は毎年休暇でプエルトリコで二週間を過ごします。 |

## Vocabulary Practice 1

▶ 8C Vocabulary Practice 1 (CD 2, Track 29)

音声を聞いて、適切な単語で空欄を埋めてください。

1. People go to stores to _____ things.

2. People usually _____ with cash or by credit card.

Around Town      **Let's Go Shopping**      What Do You Feel Like Doing?

Let's Eat!      At Work

3. Mary needs _____, so she goes to the [shoe] store.

4. John wants a new _____, so he goes to the _____.

5. People buy food at _____ stores or at

   _____.

6. Some people buy bread at a _____.

7. Some people buy meat at a _____ shop.

8. Electronics stores _____ computers, televisions, and stereos.

9. _____ stores sell paint, hammers, nails, and other things

   to fix the house.

10. _____ stores sell all kinds of things, especially

    clothes.

11. Things are _____ when they're on sale.

12. There are a lot of different stores in a _____.

13. Many people like to go _____ in malls.

14. They _____ a lot of money, and a lot of time, in malls.

答え

1. buy; 2. pay; 3. shoes, shoe; 4. book, bookstore; 5. grocery, supermarkets; 6. bakery; 7. butcher; 8. sell; 9. Hardware; 10. Department; 11. cheaper; 12. mall; 13. shopping; 14. spend

Hello! How Are You?          Big or Small? Short or Tall?          Everyday Life

This Is My Family          Welcome to My Home

# Grammar Builder 1

▶ 8D Grammar Builder 1 (CD 2, Track 30)

## 数量表現

人や数えられる物 (one person, two people; one book, three books) について質問する時は how many を使います。

| How many people are there at the store? | 店には何人の人がいますか。 |
|---|---|
| How many stores are there at the mall? | ショッピングモールには何軒の店がありますか。 |

数えられない物 (money, milk, bread, water, time) について質問する時は how much を使います。

| How much money do you spend on food every week? | 毎週どのぐらいのお金を食べ物に費やしますか。 |
|---|---|
| How much time do you spend at the store? | 店でどのぐらいの時間を費やしますか。 |

答えが zero (ゼロ)の時は no か not any を使います。

| How many people are there at the store?<br>–There are no people at the store.<br>–There aren't any people at the store. | 店には何人の人がいますか。<br>–店には誰もいません。 |
|---|---|
| How much money do you spend on magazines?<br>–I spend no money on magazines.<br>–I don't spend any money on magazines. | どのぐらいのお金を雑誌に費やしますか。<br>–雑誌には全くお金を費やしません。 |

**Essential English**

Around Town **Let's Go Shopping** What Do You Feel Like Doing?

Let's Eat! At Work

数が少ない時は数えられる名詞 (books, people, stores) の前に a few を付けます。

| You only have ten books?<br>–That's right, I only have a few books. | あなたは十冊しか本を持っていないのですか。<br>–そうです。私は数冊しか本を持っていません。 |
|---|---|
| There are only three people at the store?<br>–That's right, there are only a few people at the store. | 店には三人しかいないのですか。<br>–そうです。店には数人しかいません。 |
| The mall only has six stores?<br>–That's right, the mall only has a few stores. | ショッピングモールには六軒しか店がないのですか。<br>–そうです。ショッピングモールには数軒しか店がありません。 |

数えられない名詞 (money, time, water) の前には a little を付けます。

| You only spend five dollars on food?<br>–That's right, I only spend a little money on food. | 食べ物に5ドルしか費やさないのですか。<br>–そうです。私は食べ物には少しのお金しか費やしません。 |
|---|---|
| You only spend fifteen minutes at the store?<br>–That's right, I only spend a little time at the store. | 店には15分しかいないのですか。<br>–そうです。私は店には少しの時間しかいません。 |
| You only drink one glass of water every day?<br>–That's right, I only drink a little water every day. | 毎日水を一杯しか飲まないのですか。<br>–そうです。私は毎日少ししか水を飲みません。 |

Hello! How Are You?　　Big or Small? Short or Tall?　　Everyday Life

This Is My Family　　Welcome to My Home

数や量が多い場合は a lot of か lots of を名詞の前に付けます。

| You have five hundred books?<br>−That's right, I have a lot of books.<br>−That's right, I have lots of books. | 本を500冊持っているのですか。<br>−そうです。私はたくさんの本を持っています。 |
| You drink fifteen glasses of water a day?<br>−That's right, I drink a lot of water.<br>−That's right, I drink lots of water. | 一日に水を15杯飲むのですか。<br>−そうです。私はたくさん水を飲みます。 |

数や量が多い時は much と many を使うこともできます。数えられる名詞の前には many を、数えられない名詞の前には much を使いましょう。

| You have five hundred books?<br>−That's right, I have many books. | 本を500冊持っているのですか。<br>−そうです。私はたくさんの本を持っています。 |
| She spends four hours at the library?<br>−Yes, she spends much time at the library. | 彼女は図書館に四時間いるのですか。<br>−はい、彼女は図書館でたくさんの時間を過ごします。 |

Too much と too many は more than enough（必要十分な量よりも多い）、すなわち「多すぎる」という意味です。

| You have ten cats? You have too many cats! | 猫が10匹いるのですか。猫が多すぎますね! |
| You spend ten hours at the mall? You spend too much time shopping! | ショッピングモールに10時間いるのですか。買い物に費やす時間が多すぎますね! |

## Vocabulary Builder 2

▶ 8E Vocabulary Builder 2 (CD 2, Track 31)

| | |
|---|---|
| John and Mary need new clothes. | ジョンさんとメアリーさんは新しい洋服が必要です。 |
| They go shopping at the department store. | 彼らはデパートへ買い物に行きます。 |
| John goes to the men's department. | ジョンさんは紳士服売り場に行きます。 |
| He chooses two shirts and a pair of pants. | 彼はシャツを二枚とパンツを一枚選びます。 |
| He tries the pants on, but they're too big. | 彼はパンツを試着しますが、大きすぎます。 |
| He needs a smaller size. | 彼はもっと小さいサイズが必要です。 |
| He looks at a suit, but it's too expensive. | 彼はスーツを見ますが、高すぎます。 |
| He also chooses a jacket and a belt. | 彼はジャケットとベルトも選びます。 |
| Mary goes to the women's department. | メアリーさんは婦人服売り場に行きます。 |
| She chooses a blouse, a pair of pants, and two skirts. | 彼女はブラウスとパンツとスカートを二枚選びます。 |
| She tries on the skirts, but she doesn't like them. | 彼女はスカートを試着しますが、気に入りません。 |
| She looks at a dress and a sweater, too. | 彼女はワンピースとセーターを見ます。 |
| The dress is on sale. | ワンピースはセールになっています。 |
| The sweater is cheaper than the dress. | セーターはワンピースよりも安いです。 |

Hello! How Are You?          Big or Small? Short or Tall?          Everyday Life

This Is My Family                    Welcome to My Home

# ✎ Vocabulary Practice 2

▶ 8F Vocabulary Practice 2 (CD 3, Track 1)

音声を聞いて、空欄を適切な単語で埋めてください。

1. John and Mary _____ new clothes.

2. They _____ at the department store.

3. John goes to the men's _____.

4. He chooses two _____ and a pair of _____.

5. He tries the pants on, but they're _____.

6. He needs a _____ size.

7. He looks at a suit, but it's _____.

8. He also chooses a _____ and a _____.

9. Mary goes to the _____.

10. She chooses a _____, a pair of pants, and two _____.

11. She _____ on the skirts, but she doesn't like them.

12. She looks at a _____ and a _____, too.

13. The dress is _____.

14. The sweater is _____ than the dress.

**答え**

1. need; 2. go shopping; 3. department; 4. shirts, pants; 5. too big; 6. smaller; 7. too expensive;
8. jacket, belt; 9. women's department; 10. blouse, skirts; 11. tries; 12. dress, sweater; 13. on
sale; 14. cheaper

Around Town          **Let's Go Shopping**          What Do You Feel Like Doing?

Let's Eat!          At Work

# Grammar Builder 2

▶ 8G Grammar Builder 2 (CD 3, Track 2)

## 比較級 (BIGGER) と最上級 (BIGGEST)

二つの物や二人の人を比べる時には形容詞の語尾に –er を付けます。(old – older; young – younger)

| John is twenty-three years old, and Mary is twenty five. | ジョンさんは23歳で、メアリーさんは25歳です。 |
|---|---|
| Mary is older than John. | メアリーさんはジョンさんよりも年上です。 |
| John is younger than Mary. | ジョンさんはメアリーさんよりも年下です。 |

形容詞によっては比較級を作る時に子音を重ねなければならないものもあります。(big – bigger; hot – hotter)

| California is bigger than New Jersey. | カリフォルニアはニュージャージーよりも大きいです。 |
|---|---|
| Miami is hotter than Boston. | マイアミはボストンよりも暑いです。 |

–y で終わる形容詞は –er が語尾に付く時に y が i に変化します。(easy – easier; happy – happier)

| Algebra is easier than calculus. | 代数は微積分よりも簡単です。 |
|---|---|
| Susan is happier than Jeff. | スーザンさんはジェフさんよりも幸せです。 |

形容詞が長い場合には –er を付ける代わりに more を形容詞の前に置きます。(difficult – more difficult; expensive – more expensive; beautiful – more beautiful)

| Calculus is more difficult than algebra. | 微積分は代数よりも難しいです。 |
|---|---|

Hello! How Are You?        Big or Small? Short or Tall?        Everyday Life

This Is My Family                    Welcome to My Home

| A suit is more expensive than a shirt. | スーツはシャツよりも高いです。 |
| Is San Francisco more beautiful than Los Angeles? | サンフランシスコはロサンゼルスよりも美しいですか。 |

三つ以上の物や三人以上の人を比べるには形容詞の語尾に –est を付けます。(big – bigger – biggest; tall – taller – tallest)

| Alaska is the biggest state in the United States. | アラスカはアメリカで一番大きい州です。 |
| Mount Everest is the tallest mountain in the world. | エベレスト山は世界で一番高い山です。 |

比較級を作る時に –er の代わりに more を使わなければならない形容詞がありましたね。このような形容詞の最上級を作るには –est の代わりに the most を使います。

| This is the most expensive computer in the store. | これは店で一番高いパソコンです。 |
| What is the most beautiful city in the world? | 世界で一番美しい都市はどこですか。 |

よく使われる形容詞の中には、比較級と最上級が不規則なものがあります。(good – better – best; bad – worse – worst)

| Mary is a better student than Peter, but Sam is the best student in the class. | メアリーさんはピーターさんよりも良い学生ですが、サムさんがクラスで一番の学生です。 |
| This is the cheapest computer in the store, but it's also the worst. | これは店で一番安いパソコンですが、一番悪いパソコンでもあります。 |

more の反意語は less で、the most の反意語は the least です。

| The red shirt costs fifty dollars, and the blue shirt costs forty dollars, so the blue shirt is less expensive than the red shirt. | 赤いシャツは50ドルで、青いシャツは40ドルなので、青いシャツの方が赤いシャツよりも安いです。 |

**Essential English**

Around Town     **Let's Go Shopping**     What Do You Feel Like Doing?

Let's Eat!     At Work

| The green shirt costs thirty dollars; it's the least expensive shirt. | 緑のシャツは30ドルです。これは一番安いシャツです。 |

**too** は more than enough（必要十分な量よりも多い）、すなわち「〜すぎる」という意味であることを覚えておきましょう。

| I need a size 10 shoe. This is a size 9; it's too small. | サイズ10の靴が必要です。これはサイズ9です。小さすぎます。 |
| That shirt is one hundred dollars? That's too expensive! | あのシャツは100ドルなのですか？それは高すぎます！ |

# ✎ Work Out 1

▶ 8H Work Out 1 (CD 3, Track 3)

音声を聞いて空欄を埋めてください。

1. Russia is the _____ country in the world.

2. Is your computer _____ than my computer?

3. This shirt is _____ small; I need a _____ size.

4. The Thai restaurant is _____ than the Italian restaurant.

5. Is a dress _____ than a skirt?

6. Who is the _____ professor at the university?

7. Today is the _____ day of the year.

8. This is the _____ class!

9. Clothes in this store are _____ than clothes at the mall.

10. They live in the _____ house on the street.

11. My car is _____ than your car.

だいいっか 8: Let's Go Shopping     **151**

Hello! How Are You?    Big or Small? Short or Tall?    Everyday Life

This Is My Family    Welcome to My Home

**12.** That is the _____ book in the library!

**答え**

1. biggest; 2. newer; 3. too, bigger; 4. better; 5. more expensive; 6. best; 7. longest; 8. most difficult; 9. cheaper; 10. smallest; 11. less expensive; 12. least interesting

## 🎧 Bring It All Together

▶ 8I Bring It All Together (CD 3, Track 4)

ジャックさんとメリッサさんは洋服を買おうとしています。二人の会話を聞いてみましょう。

| | |
|---|---|
| Jack: | **What do you think about this blue shirt?** |
| ジャック: | この青いシャツをどう思う? |
| Melissa: | **Not bad … It's better than the red shirt.** |
| メリッサ: | 悪くないわ・・・赤いシャツよりはいいわね。 |
| Jack: | **Yeah, but it's more expensive, too.** |
| ジャック: | うん、でも赤いシャツよりも高いけどね。 |
| Melissa: | **Well, better clothes cost more.** |
| メリッサ: | いい洋服の方がお金がかかるものよ。 |
| Jack: | **Oh, come on. That's not true. Some cheap clothes are good.** |
| ジャック: | いやいや、そんなことないよ。安い洋服でもいいものはあるよ。 |
| Melissa: | **Not many! But the blue shirt is nice. It's the nicest shirt in the store.** |
| メリッサ: | そんなに多くはないわ!それはそうと、青いシャツはいいと思う。この店で一番いいシャツだわ。 |
| Jack: | **Great. I'll get it. But I need a pair of pants, too.** |
| ジャック: | うん。買うよ。でもパンツも要るんだ。 |
| Melissa: | **Do you want jeans? They sell really great jeans here.** |
| メリッサ: | ジーンズは欲しい?ここではとてもいいジーンズを売ってるわ。 |
| Jack: | **Not jeans; something less casual. I need them for work.** |
| ジャック: | ジーンズは要らないよ。そんなにカジュアルじゃないものが欲しいね。仕事用に必要なんだ。 |

| Melissa: | Here. How about these gray pants? |
| メリッサ: | はい、これ。このグレーのパンツはどう？ |
| Jack: | They're nice! What size are they? |
| ジャック: | これいいね！サイズは？ |
| Melissa: | Thirty-one. |
| メリッサ: | 31よ。 |
| Jack: | That's too small. I wear thirty-two. |
| ジャック: | それじゃ小さすぎだよ。僕は32なんだ。 |
| Melissa: | Ah, here we go. Size thirty-two. |
| メリッサ: | それじゃ、これをどうぞ。32よ。 |
| Jack: | But how much do they cost? |
| ジャック: | いくら？ |
| Melissa: | I don't know. I don't see any price tag. Oh, here it is. Sixty dollars. And look, they're on sale. Twenty percent off! |
| メリッサ: | 分からないわ。値札が見当たらない。ああ、ここにあったわ。60ドル。ねえ見て、セールになってるわ。20パーセントオフよ！ |
| Jack: | That's not bad! Forty dollars! |
| ジャック: | 悪くないね！40ドルかあ！ |
| Melissa: | Forty dollars? You mean forty-eight dollars. I hope your cooking is better than your math. |
| メリッサ: | 40ドル？48ドルでしょ。あなたの料理の腕前は算数よりはマシだと願うわ。 |
| Jack: | Oops, yeah. My math is much worse than my cooking. Why? |
| ジャック: | あっ。うん、まあ僕は料理よりも算数の方がずっとダメだけど。なんで？ |
| Melissa: | Because I'm hungry, and you're cooking dinner tonight. |
| メリッサ: | お腹が空いてるから。そして今夜はあなたが夕飯を作るからよ。 |

## ✏ Work Out 2

適切な単語を選んでください。

1. How (much/many) shirts do you have?

Hello! How Are You?          Big or Small? Short or Tall?          Everyday Life

This Is My Family                    Welcome to My Home

2. They only have a (little/few) money.

3. There aren't (some/any) good clothing stores at the mall.

4. We have a (little/few) pairs of pants in size thirty-two.

5. You eat too (much/many) sugar!

6. There are (much/many) good restaurants in the city.

7. We don't have (some/any) more blouses in your size.

8. How (much/many) water do you drink every day?

9. They have (some/any) nice belts in the men's department.

10. We don't have (much/many) time for shopping today.

**答え**
1. many; 2. little; 3. any; 4. few; 5. much; 6. many; 7. any; 8. much; 9. some; 10. much

正しい形容詞の形を選んでください。

1. Billy is the _____ boy in the class.

   a. taller

   b. tallest

   c. most tall

   d. more tall

2. Is the Nile _____ than the Amazon?

   a. longest

   b. long

   c. most long

   d. longer

**Essential English**

Around Town      **Let's Go Shopping**      What Do You Feel Like Doing?

Let's Eat!      At Work

3. This belt is _____ than the shirt.

   a. more expensive

   b. most expensive

   c. the most expensive

   d. expensive

4. This is the _____ clothing store in the mall.

   a. good

   b. better

   c. most good

   d. best

5. I need a _____ computer.

   a. faster

   b. most fast

   c. fastest

   d. more fast

6. The dress is very _____.

   a. more beautiful

   b. less beautiful

   c. beautiful

   d. most beautiful

7. Do you have a _____ size?

   a. smallest

Hello! How Are You?    Big or Small? Short or Tall?    Everyday Life

This Is My Family    Welcome to My Home

b. smaller

c. least small

d. more small

8. Who is _____, Jack or Dan?

a. old

b. oldest

c. more old

d. older

9. Her question is very _____.

a. more difficult

b. most difficult

c. difficult

d. the most difficult

10. This is the _____ pair of pants in the store.

a. cheap

b. more cheap

c. cheaper

d. cheapest

答え
1. b; 2. d; 3. a; 4. d; 5. a; 6. c; 7. b; 8. d; 9. c; 10. d

# ✎ Drive It Home

much や many など、数量を表す言葉を練習してみましょう。まずは、
How much ... is there? あるいは How many ... are there? のどちらか適切な形式
を用いて数量を尋ねる疑問文を作ってください。

Around Town      **Let's Go Shopping**      What Do You Feel Like Doing?

Let's Eat!      At Work

1. coffee

   _____

2. shoes

   _____

3. electronics stores

   _____

4. time

   _____

5. sugar

   _____

6. people

   _____

7. shirts

   _____

8. money

   _____

9. pairs of pants

   _____

10. water

   _____

答え

1. How much coffee is there? 2. How many shoes are there? 3. How many electronics stores are there? 4. How much time is there? 5. How much sugar is there? 6. How many people are there? 7. How many shirts are there? 8. How much money is there? 9. How many pairs of pants are

Hello! How Are You?     Big or Small? Short or Tall?     Everyday Life

This Is My Family     Welcome to My Home

there? 10. How much water is there?

今度は **There is a little ...** または **There are a few ...** のどちらか適切な形式を用いて数量を表す文章を作ってください。

1. milk

   _____

2. skirts

   _____

3. forks

   _____

4. food

   _____

5. students

   _____

6. clothing stores

   _____

7. time

   _____

8. belts

   _____

9. coffee

   _____

Around Town      **Let's Go Shopping**      What Do You Feel Like Doing?

Let's Eat!      At Work

10. **pairs of shoes**

---

**答え**

1. There is a little milk. 2. There are a few skirts. 3. There are a few forks. 4. There is a little food. 5. There are a few students. 6. There are a few clothing stores. 7. There is a little time. 8. There are a few belts. 9. There is a little coffee. 10. There are a few pairs of shoes.

# Parting Words

**Congratulations!**（おめでとうございます！）これで第8課は終了です。学習した内容を確認しましょう。

☐ 店の名前や買い物に関する語彙 （まだ自信がない場合は p.141 に戻って復習しましょう。）

☐ **many** や **much** といった数量を表す言葉 （まだ自信がない場合は p.144 に戻って復習しましょう。）

☐ **clothing**（衣服）の種類 （まだ自信がない場合は p.147 に戻って復習しましょう。）

☐ 比較級（**bigger** など）と最上級（**biggest** など） （まだ自信がない場合は p.149 に戻って復習しましょう。）

☐ 買い物に関する会話の中で学習した項目を総合的に使う （まだ自信がない場合は p.152 に戻って復習しましょう。）

www.livinglanguage.com/languagelab のページをチェックするのを忘れずに。バーチャル単語帳やゲームやクイズで、学習したことを復習してみましょう！

# Word Recall

第8課で学習した単語を覚えているか確認しましょう。

A.

1. What do people usually do at stores?

   _____

2. If you don't have cash, you can pay by ...

   _____

3. Where do you buy shoes?

   _____

4. Where do you buy books?

   _____

5. Where do you buy food?

   _____

6. Where do some people buy bread and cakes?

   _____

7. Where do some people buy meat?

   _____

8. What kind of store sells computers, televisions, and stereos?

   _____

**Essential English**

9. What kind of store sells paint, hammers, nails, and other things to fix the house?

_____

10. Are things cheaper or more expensive when they're on sale?

_____

11. What do you call a place with a lot of different stores?

_____

B.

1. If a pair of pants is too big, you need a _____ size.

2. If a sweater is too expensive, you need something _____.

3. Before you buy new clothes, you try them _____.

答え:
A. 1. They buy things. They go shopping. 2. credit card; 3. at a shoe store; 4. at a bookstore; 5. at a supermarket または grocery store; 6. at a bakery (または supermarket); 7. at a butcher shop (または supermarket); 8. an electronics store (または department store); 9. hardware store; 10. They're cheaper. 11. a mall
B. 1. smaller; 2. cheaper (または less expensive); 3. on

Hello! How Are You?　　　　Big or Small? Short or Tall?　　　　Everyday Life

This Is My Family　　　　　　Welcome to My Home

# だいいっか 9: 職場で

**Lesson 9: At Work**

**Hello!**（こんにちは！）本課では仕事 (work) についての話題を扱います。学習内容は以下の通りです。

☐ 仕事や職業の名前

☐ **want to, have to, can, must, should, need to** の使い方

☐ 仕事や職場について話す時に必要な語彙

☐ **is working, am going, are taking** といった現在進行形

☐ オフィスでの会話の中で学習した項目を総合的に使う
　　まずは語彙から始めましょう。

# Vocabulary Builder 1

▶ 9A Vocabulary Builder 1 (CD 3, Track 5)

| | |
|---|---|
| A teacher works in a school and teaches students. | 先生は学校で働き、生徒に教えます。 |
| A professor works at a university and teaches students. | 教授は大学で働き、生徒に教えます。 |
| A doctor works at a hospital and treats sick people. | 医者は病院で働き、病人を治療します。 |
| A nurse also works at a hospital and helps doctors and sick people. | 看護師も病院で働き、医者や病人を助けます。 |
| A lawyer works at a law firm and practices law. | 弁護士は法律事務所で働き、弁護士業を行います。 |
| A plumber comes to your house and repairs the sink or toilet. | 配管工は家に来て、流し台やトイレの修理をします。 |
| An architect designs houses and office buildings. | 建築家は家やオフィスビルの設計をします。 |
| A construction worker builds houses and other buildings. | 建設作業員は家やビルを建てます。 |
| An engineer designs bridges, highways, and other big projects. | エンジニアは橋や高速道路やその他大きなプロジェクトの設計をします。 |
| A carpenter works with wood and makes tables, chairs, cabinets, and other things. | 大工は木を使ってテーブルや椅子や棚などを作ります。 |
| A factory worker works in a factory and makes cars or other products. | 工場作業員は工場で働き、車やその他の製品を作ります。 |
| A mail carrier delivers your mail. | 郵便配達員は郵便を配達します。 |
| A salesperson works in a store and sells things. | 販売員は店で働き、物を売ります。 |

Hello! How Are You?    Big or Small? Short or Tall?    Everyday Life

This Is My Family    Welcome to My Home

| A cook works in a restaurant and prepares food. | 調理師はレストランで働き、食事を作ります。 |
| An office manager organizes an office. | オフィスマネージャーはオフィス事務を管理します。 |
| A secretary answers the phone in an office, writes reports, and does many other things. | 秘書はオフィスで電話の応答をしたり、レポートを書いたり、その他多くのことをします。 |
| A police officer protects people and fights crime. | 警察官は人々を守り、犯罪と戦います。 |
| A fire fighter puts out fires. | 消防士は火を消します。 |

# ✎ Vocabulary Practice 1

職業とその説明を正しく組み合わせてください。

1. A teacher …

2. A nurse …

3. A lawyer …

4. An engineer …

5. A plumber …

6. A mail carrier …

7. An architect …

a. designs bridges, highways, and other big projects.

b. works with wood and makes tables, chairs, cabinets, and other things.

c. works at a hospital and treats sick people.

d. answers the phone in an office, writes reports, and does many other things.

e. works at a university and teaches students.

f. works at a hospital and helps doctors and sick people.

g. protects people and fights crime.

**Essential English**

8. A construction worker ...

h. comes to your house and repairs the sink or toilet.

9. A carpenter ...

i. works in a store and sells things.

10. A secretary ...

j. works at a law firm and practices law.

11. A doctor ...

k. builds houses and other buildings.

12. A factory worker ...

l. puts out fires.

13. A salesperson ...

m. designs houses and office buildings.

14. A professor ...

n. organizes an office.

15. A cook ...

o. works in a school and teaches students.

16. An office manager ...

p. works in a restaurant and prepares food.

17. A fire fighter ...

q. works in a factory and makes cars or other products.

18. A police officer ...

r. delivers your mail.

**答え**

1. o; 2. f; 3. j; 4. a; 5. h; 6. r; 7. m; 8. k; 9. b; 10. d; 11. c; 12. q; 13. i; 14. e; 15. p; 16. n; 17. l; 18. g

# Grammar Builder 1

▶ 9B Grammar Builder 1 (CD 3, Track 6)

## WANT TO, HAVE TO, CAN, MUST, SHOULD, NEED TO

want to, have to, can, must, should, need to を使う時は他の動詞が後に続きます。例えば、want to eat, have to study, can speak, should drink, needs to go といったようになります。

Hello! How Are You?        Big or Small? Short or Tall?        Everyday Life

This Is My Family                    Welcome to My Home

want to は「〜したい」という意味です。主語が he/she/it の時は want to の代わりに wants to を使います。否定形は don't want to または doesn't want to です。

| I'm hungry. I want to eat. | お腹が空いています。食べたいです。 |
|---|---|
| Bill doesn't like his job. He wants to get a new job. | ビルさんは自分の仕事が好きではありません。彼は新しい仕事に就きたがっています。 |
| We don't like pizza. We don't want to eat pizza. | 私達はピザが好きではありません。私達はピザを食べたくありません。 |

can は可能を表します。主語が he/she/it の時でも –s は付きません。Can の否定形は can't または cannot です。

| George knows English, Japanese, and Russian. He can speak three languages. | ジョージさんは英語と日本語とロシア語が分かります。彼は三ヶ国語が話せます。 |
|---|---|
| I don't speak Chinese, so I can't understand Li. | 私は中国語を話しませんから、リーさんの言うことを理解できません。 |
| We don't have any money, so we cannot buy a new car. | 私達はお金が全くないので、新しい車を買えません。 |

have to は「〜しなければならない」という意味です。主語が he/she/it の時は has to を使います。否定形は don't have to または doesn't have to です。

| It's eight thirty; I have to leave for work. | 今8時30分です。仕事に行かなければなりません。 |
|---|---|
| Barbara has a test tomorrow; she has to study tonight. | バーバラさんは明日テストがあります。今夜勉強しなければなりません。 |
| Tomorrow is Saturday, so we don't have to work. | 明日は土曜日ですから、私達は仕事をしなくてもいいです。 |

**Essential English**

**Must** は **have to** と似ていますが、少し格式ばった言い方にしたい時、あるいは切迫した様子を表したい時に使います。主語が **he/she/it** の時でも **must** に **–s** は付きません。

| It's eight thirty. I must leave for work. | 今8時30分です。仕事に行かなければなりません。 |
| Barbara has a test tomorrow; she must study tonight. | バーバラさんは明日テストがあります。今夜勉強しなければなりません。 |

**Must not** と **don't/doesn't have to** では意味が違いますので注意しましょう。

| It's Saturday. You don't have to go to work today. You can stay home. | 今日は土曜日です。今日あなたは仕事に行かなくてもいいです。家にいることができます。 |
| You're sick! You must not go to work today! You have to stay home. | あなたは具合が悪いです！今日仕事に行ってはいけません。家にいなくてはいけません。 |

**should** は「〜するべきだ」という意味です。主語が **he/she/it** の時でも **–s** は付きません。否定形は **shouldn't** です。

| You don't drink enough water. You should drink more water. | あなたは十分な量の水を飲みません。もっと水を飲むべきです。 |
| It's late and we have to work tomorrow. We should go home now. | もう遅いし、明日仕事をしなければなりません。もう家に帰るべきです。 |
| You shouldn't smoke! It's bad for you. | 煙草は吸わないべきです！身体に悪いですよ。 |

**need to** は「〜する必要がある」という意味です。主語が **he/she/it** の時は **needs to** になります。否定形は **don't need to** あるいは **doesn't need to** です。

| My computer doesn't work. I need to buy a new computer. | 私のパソコンは壊れています。新しいパソコンを買う必要があります。 |

Hello! How Are You?    Big or Small? Short or Tall?    Everyday Life

This Is My Family    Welcome to My Home

| I have a test tomorrow. I need to study. | 私は明日テストがあります。勉強する必要があります。 |
| You don't need to pay with cash. You can pay with your credit card. | 現金で支払う必要はありません。クレジットカードで支払えますよ。 |

疑問文では can と must と should は主語の前に来ます。

| Can you speak Polish? | あなたはポーランド語を話せますか。 |
| How many languages can you speak? | あなたは何ヶ国語を話せますか。 |
| Why must you speak with her secretary? | どうしてあなたは彼女の秘書と話さなければならないのですか。 |
| Should we stay home or go to a restaurant? | 家にいるべきでしょうか、それともレストランに行くべきでしょうか。 |

want to と have to と need to で疑問文を作る時は do か does を一緒に使います。

| Do you want to go to the library with me tomorrow? | 明日私と図書館に行きたいですか。 |
| Does Mary have to work next week? | メアリーさんは来週仕事をしなければいけませんか。 |
| Do I need to pay with cash, or can I use my credit card? | 現金で支払わなければなりませんか。それともクレジットカードを使えますか。 |

# Vocabulary Builder 2

▶ 9C Vocabulary Builder 2 (CD 3, Track 7)

| Jack works in an office. | ジャックさんはオフィスで働きます。 |
| He works from nine o'clock to five o'clock, from Monday to Friday. | 彼は月曜日から金曜日まで、9時から5時まで働きます。 |
| He works for Gloria Peterson; she is his boss. | 彼はグロリア・ピーターソンさんのもとで働いています。彼女は彼の上司です。 |

| Jack is Gloria's assistant. | ジャックさんはグロリアさんのアシスタントです。 |
| He answers her phone and takes messages when she isn't in her office. | 彼女がオフィスを留守にしている時に、彼は電話に出たり伝言を受けたりします。 |
| He organizes her meetings. | 彼は彼女のミーティングを管理します。 |
| When someone wants to see her, he schedules an appointment. | 誰かが彼女に会いたい時は、彼がミーティングの日時を設定します。 |
| He updates her calendar with new meetings. | 彼は新しいミーティングを彼女のカレンダーに追加します。 |
| Jack works on his computer most of the time. | ジャックさんはほとんどパソコンで仕事をします。 |
| He sends e-mails, writes reports, and makes photocopies. | 彼はメールを送信したり、レポートを書いたり、コピーをとったりします。 |
| Jack has a lunch break at twelve thirty every day. | ジャックさんは毎日12時30分に昼休みをとります。 |
| It's twelve forty now, so Jack is not working. | 今12時40分ですので、ジャックさんは働いていません。 |
| He is eating lunch with his coworkers. | 彼は同僚と一緒に昼ご飯を食べています。 |

# ✎ Vocabulary Practice 2

▶ 9D Vocabulary Practice 2 (CD 3, Track 8)

新出ボキャブラリーの練習です。音声を聞いて空欄を適切な動詞で埋めてください。

1. Jack _____ in an office.

Hello! How Are You?        Big or Small? Short or Tall?        Everyday Life

This Is My Family                    Welcome to My Home

1. He works _____ nine o'clock to five o'clock, from Monday _____ Friday.

2. He works _____ Gloria Peterson; she is his _____.

3. Jack is Gloria's _____.

4. He _____ her phone and takes _____ when she isn't in her office.

5. He organizes her _____.

6. When someone wants to see her, he _____ an _____.

7. He updates her _____ with new meetings.

8. Jack works _____ his computer _____ of the time.

9. He _____ e-mails, _____ reports, and _____ photocopies.

10. Jack has a lunch break at twelve thirty _____ day.

11. It's twelve forty _____, so Jack is not _____.

12. He is _____ lunch with his coworkers.

答え

1. works; 2. from, to; 3. for, boss; 4. assistant; 5. answers, messages; 6. meetings; 7. schedules, appointment; 8. calendar; 9. on, most; 10. sends; writes, makes; 11. every; 12. now, working; 13. eating

## Grammar Builder 2

▶ 9E Grammar Builder 2 (CD 3, Track 9)

### 現在進行形: IS WORKING, AM GOING, ARE TAKING

第5課では I work, you work, he works, she works といった単純現在形を学習しました。単純現在形は usually, on Tuesdays, at nine o'clock, every day, in the afternoons, always, generally, never などの時を表す表現と一緒に使うことができます。

| Jack works on Mondays, Tuesdays, Wednesdays, Thursdays, and Fridays. | ジャックさんは月曜日、火曜日、水曜日、木曜日、そして金曜日に働きます。 |
| --- | --- |
| Jack never works on Saturday or Sunday. | ジャックさんは土曜日と日曜日には働きません。 |
| He usually gets to work at nine o'clock. | 彼はたいてい9時に出勤します。 |
| But sometimes he gets to work at eight thirty. | けれども彼は時々8時30分に出勤します。 |
| He always eats lunch at twelve thirty. | 彼はいつも12時30分に昼ご飯を食べます。 |

それに対して現在進行形 (–ing) は今起こっていることを表現します。

| Today is Monday, so Jack is working. | 今日は月曜日ですから、ジャックさんは働いています。 |
| --- | --- |
| Today is Saturday, so Jack is not working. | 今日は土曜日ですから、ジャックさんは働いていません。 |
| It's nine o'clock, so Jack is walking into the office. | 今9時ですから、ジャックさんはオフィスに入るところです。 |
| It's twelve thirty, so Jack is eating lunch. | 今12時30分ですから、ジャックさんは昼ご飯を食べています。 |

Hello! How Are You?　　　Big or Small? Short or Tall?　　　Everyday Life

This Is My Family　　　Welcome to My Home

現在進行形は be 動詞 (am, is, are) + 本動詞 + –ing で作ります。

| | |
|---|---|
| **I am working**<br>私は働いています | **we are working**<br>私達は働いています |
| **you are working**<br>あなたは働いています | **you are working**<br>あなた達は働いています |
| **he/she/it is working**<br>彼/彼女/それは働いています | **they are working**<br>彼ら(彼女ら/それら)は働いています |

否定形を作るときは not を本動詞の前に付けます。

| | |
|---|---|
| **I am not eating**<br>私は食べていません | **we are not eating**<br>私達は食べていません |
| **you are not eating**<br>あなたは食べていません | **you are not eating**<br>あなた達は食べていません |
| **he/she/it is not eating**<br>彼/彼女/それは食べていません | **they are not eating**<br>彼ら(彼女ら/それら)は食べていません |

be 動詞の否定形は短縮することができましたね。(**you're not/ you aren't, he's not/ he isn't** など)

| | |
|---|---|
| **I'm not sleeping**<br>私は寝ていません | **we're not sleeping/we aren't sleeping**<br>私達は寝ていません |
| **you're not sleeping/your aren't sleeping**<br>あなたは寝ていません | **you're not sleeping/you aren't sleeping**<br>あなた達は寝ていません |
| **he's not sleeping/he isn't sleeping**<br>彼は寝ていません<br>**she's not sleeping/she isn't sleeping**<br>彼女は寝ていません | **they're not sleeping/they aren't sleeping**<br>彼ら(彼女ら)は寝ていません |

　　**Essential English**

疑問文を作るときは am, is, are が主語の前に置かれます。

| Are you working now? | 今あなたは働いていますか。 |
| Is she eating lunch with her coworkers? | 彼女は同僚と昼ご飯を食べていますか。 |
| What is he saying? I can't hear. | 彼は何と言っているのですか。聞こえません。 |

現在形を使って、近い将来について話すこともできます。そのような時は tonight, tomorrow, next week といった時を表す表現がよく一緒に使われます。

| We're going to a new restaurant tonight. | 私達は今夜新しいレストランに行きます。 |
| Are you working tomorrow, or do you have the day off? | あなたは明日仕事をしますか。それともお休みですか。 |
| They're meeting next week. | 彼らは来週に会います。 |

現在進行形を作る時、動詞の綴りについて注意する点があります。動詞が –e で終わる場合は –e を消してから –ing を付けます (例: come – coming; take – taking)。動詞の語尾が子音一音の場合は、その子音を重ねてから –ing を付けます (例: get – getting; put – putting)。動詞の語尾が –ie の場合は –ie を –y に変えてから –ing を付けます (例: lie – lying; die – dying)。動詞の語尾が y の場合は何も変える必要はありません (例: try – trying; copy – copying)。

# ✎ Work Out 1
▶ 9F Work Out 1 (CD 3, Track 10)

音声を聞いて空欄を埋めてください。

1. We _____ speak with your boss.

2. Does he _____ go to work tomorrow morning?

Hello! How Are You?   Big or Small? Short or Tall?   Everyday Life

This Is My Family   Welcome to My Home

3. What _____ I say to Mrs. Jenson?

4. We _____ finish the report today.

5. _____ you understand the question?

6. You're sick; you _____ to work today.

7. Bill _____ a new job soon.

8. She _____ the telephone.

9. You _____ jeans to the office.

10. Where _____ work?

**答え**

1. want to; 2. have to; 3. should; 4. don't have to; 5. Can; 6. must not go; 7. needs to find; 8. can't hear; 9. shouldn't wear; 10. do you want to

## 🎧 Bring It All Together

▶ 9G Bring It All Together (CD 3, Track 11)

マークさんとスーさんは同じ会社で働いています。二人はオフィスで何かを話しているようです。聞いてみましょう。

| | |
|---|---|
| **Mark:** | **Hey, Sue! What are you doing?** |
| マーク: | やあ、スー!何してるの? |
| **Sue:** | **I'm finishing a report for my boss. What are you doing?** |
| スー: | 上司に提出するレポートを仕上げているところよ。あなたは何してるの? |
| **Mark:** | **I'm leaving for lunch. Do you want to come?** |
| マーク: | ランチに行くところなんだ。君も来る? |
| **Sue:** | **Oh, sorry. I can't leave right now.** |
| スー: | ああ、ごめんなさい。今は出られないわ。 |
| **Mark:** | **Why not? It's twelve thirty.** |
| マーク: | なんで?12時半だよ。 |

**Sue:** Yeah, but I'm going to a meeting in ten minutes.
スー: うん、でもあと10分で会議に行くのよ。

**Mark:** Oh, too bad. Don't you usually have lunch at twelve thirty?
マーク: それは残念だ。普段12時半に昼ご飯を食べるんじゃなかった？

**Sue:** Yes, I usually eat at twelve thirty, but today I have an important meeting. So I have to stay at the office and eat later.
スー: ええ、普段は12時半に食べるけど、今日は重要な会議があるのよ。だからオフィスに残って、食べるのは後にしないといけないわ。

**Mark:** Well, what are you doing tonight after work?
マーク: じゃあ、今夜会社の後は何するの？

**Sue:** Tonight? I have to work until six, but I don't have any plans after that. Why? What's going on?
スー: 今夜？6時まで仕事しないといけないけど、その後は特に予定はないわ。なんで？何かあるの？

**Mark:** It's Bill's birthday, so a few of us are going to dinner. You should come.
マーク: 今日はビルの誕生日なんだよ。だから何人かで夕飯に行くんだ。君もおいでよ。

**Sue:** Today's Bill's birthday? I want to come, but I have to come into the office early tomorrow. My boss needs to have my report by nine, so I'll need to work on it tomorrow morning.
スー: 今日はビルの誕生日なの？行きたいけれど、明日は早く出社しないといけないの。9時までに上司にレポートを提出するのよ。だから明日の朝レポートを終わらせないと。

**Mark:** No problem. We're having dinner at seven. So you can be home by eleven.
マーク: 心配いらないよ。ディナーは7時だから、11時までには帰宅できるよ。

**Sue:** Eleven? That's a long dinner! You're eating from seven until eleven?
スー: 11時？随分長いディナーなのね！7時から11時まで食べてるの？

**Mark:** No. After dinner we're probably seeing a movie. But you don't have to come to the movies if you need to get home early.

Hello! How Are You?          Big or Small? Short or Tall?          Everyday Life

This Is My Family                Welcome to My Home

| | |
|---|---|
| マーク: | いや、ご飯のあと、多分映画を見ると思う。でも早く家に帰らないといけないようなら、映画には来なくていいよ。 |
| Sue: | That sounds good. I can meet all of you for dinner, but I should leave by eight thirty. |
| スー: | それならいいわ。みんなとディナーは一緒できるわ。でも8時半までに出ないとだめね。 |
| Mark: | Perfect. After lunch, look for an e-mail from me with the address of the restaurant. |
| マーク: | いいよ。ランチの後、レストランの住所を書いてメールを送るから見てね。 |
| Sue: | Okay. Have a great lunch, and I'll see you later tonight. |
| スー: | オーケー。ランチを楽しんで。それじゃ今夜ね。 |

## ✎ Work Out 2

want to, have to, can, must, should, need to の練習をしましょう。適切な言葉を選んでください。

1. Greg speaks Spanish and English. He (should/can) speak two languages.

2. It's late and I'm working tomorrow. I (can/need to) get home.

3. You don't eat enough vegetables. You (want to/should) eat more vegetables.

4. Tomorrow is Saturday and I'm not working, so I (don't have to/must not) get home early tonight.

5. Julia's car is old and ugly. She (wants to/can) buy a new car.

6. We don't have very much money, so we (don't want to/can't) go to an expensive restaurant.

7. It's eight thirty and Bill starts work at nine o'clock. He (wants to/has to) leave for work.

**Essential English**

8. It's cold outside! You (don't have to/must not) go outside without a jacket.

9. The music is too loud. We (can't/shouldn't) hear you.

10. Carla doesn't like her job. She (can/wants to) find a new one.

**答え**
1. can; 2. need to; 3. should; 4. don't have to; 5. wants to; 6. can't; 7. has to; 8. must not; 9. can't; 10. wants to

次は単純現在形と現在進行形のどちらかを選んでください。

1. They (watch/are watching) television right now.

2. I usually (get/am getting) to work at eight forty-five in the morning.

3. Doctors (work/are working) in hospitals.

4. The nurse (helps/is helping) the doctor with a patient now.

5. What (do you do/are you doing) later tonight?

6. Where (do they go/are they going) for vacation every year?

7. The plumber (doesn't work/isn't working) on Sundays.

8. Who (goes/is going) to the movies with you this weekend?

9. I can't hear. What (do they say/are they saying)?

10. My father (goes/is going) to the office sometimes on Saturday mornings.

**答え**
1. are watching; 2. get; 3. work; 4. is helping; 5. are you doing; 6. do they go; 7. doesn't work; 8. is going; 9. are they saying; 10. goes

Hello! How Are You?       Big or Small? Short or Tall?       Everyday Life

This Is My Family       Welcome to My Home

# ✎ Drive It Home

それぞれの文の動詞を単純現在形から現在進行形に変えてください。

例: **I drink a cup of coffee.**
答え: **I'm drinking a cup of coffee.**

1. **The plumber comes to their house.**

   _____

2. **We eat dinner at a Japanese restaurant.**

   _____

3. **They speak to their bosses.**

   _____

4. **The kids sleep in their bedroom.**

   _____

5. **I have breakfast with my family.**

   _____

6. **The engineer designs a bridge.**

   _____

7. **The salesperson helps the customer.**

   _____

8. **The construction workers build an apartment building.**

   _____

**答え**

1. The plumber is coming to their house. 2. We're eating dinner at a Japanese restaurant.
3. They're speaking to their bosses. 4. The kids are sleeping in their bedroom. 5. I'm having

**Essential English**

breakfast with my family. 6. The engineer is designing a bridge. 7. The salesperson is helping the customer. 8. The construction workers are building an apartment building.

## Parting Words

Terrific!（素晴らしいです！）第9課が終了しました。Essential English も 残すところもう1課で終わりです。本課で学習した内容を確認しましょう。

□ 仕事や職業の名前　（まだ自信がない場合は p.163 に戻って復習しましょう。）

□ want to, have to, can, must, should, need to の使い方　（まだ自信がない場合は p.165 に戻って復習しましょう。）

□ 仕事や職場について話す時に必要な語彙　（まだ自信がない場合は p.168 に戻って復習しましょう。）

□ is working, am going, are taking といった現在進行形　（まだ自信がない場合は p.171 に戻って復習しましょう。）

□ オフィスでの会話の中で学習した項目を総合的に使う　（まだ自信がない場合は p.174 に戻って復習しましょう。）

www.livinglanguage.com/languagelab のページをチェックするのを忘れずに。バーチャル単語帳やゲームやクイズで、学習したことを復習してみましょう！

# Word Recall

職業を表す語彙の復習です。

1. Who works in a school with students? _____

2. Who teaches at a university? _____

3. Who comes to your house and repairs the sink or toilet? _____

4. Who protects people and fights crime? _____

5. Who works at a hospital and treats sick people? _____

6. Who delivers your mail? _____

7. Who works with wood and makes tables, chairs, and cabinets? _____

8. Who works at a law firm and practices law? _____

9. Who works in a restaurant and prepares food? _____

10. Who designs houses and office buildings? _____

11. Who answers the phone in an office and writes reports? _____

12. Who builds houses and other buildings? _____

13. Who works in a hospital and helps doctors and sick people? _____

14. Who puts out fires? _____

15. Who works in a store and sells things? _____

16. Who organizes an office? _____

**Essential English**

17. Who designs bridges, highways, and other big projects? _____

18. Who works in a factory and makes cars or other products? _____

Hello! How Are You?　　　Big or Small? Short or Tall?　　　Everyday Life

This Is My Family　　　Welcome to My Home

# だいいっか 10: 何をしたい気分ですか。

## Lesson 10: What Do You Feel Like Doing?

**Hi there!**（こんにちは！）いよいよ *Essential English* の最終レッスンになりました。おめでとうございます！ 本課では趣味や余暇についての話題を扱います。学習内容は以下の通りです。

☐ 趣味に関する語彙

☐ 好き (**like**) 嫌い (**don't like**) について話す

☐ 余暇の過ごし方に関する語彙

☐ 指示詞 **this** と **that**

☐ 週末の計画についての会話の中で学習した項目を総合的に使う
さあ始めましょう。

## Vocabulary Builder 1

▶ 10A Vocabulary Builder 1 (CD 3, Track 12)

| What are your hobbies? | あなたの趣味は何ですか。 |
|---|---|
| I like cooking and reading. | 私は料理と読書が好きです。 |
| I like to go horseback riding. | 私は乗馬をするのが好きです。 |
| We love to go hiking in the mountains. | 私達は山へハイキングに行くのが大好きです。 |
| We also like to go camping. | 私達はキャンプに行くのも好きです。 |
| Bill loves to bike. | ビルさんはサイクリングが大好きです。 |
| Sue likes to go running. | スーさんは走りに行くのが好きです。 |
| Greg loves to play guitar, but Diane prefers to play piano. | グレッグさんはギターを弾くのが大好きですが、ダイアンさんはピアノを弾く方が好きです。 |
| Nicole enjoys sewing. | ニコルさんは裁縫を楽しみます。 |
| Do you like collecting stamps or coins? | あなたは切手やコインを集めるのが好きですか。 |
| My parents like to take long walks. | 私の両親は長距離の散歩に出掛けるのが好きです。 |
| Eddie likes to draw. | エディーさんは絵を書くのが好きです。 |
| We enjoy boating during the summer. | 私達は夏の間ボート漕ぎを楽しみます。 |

## ✎ Vocabulary Practice 1

▶ 10B Vocabulary Practice 1 (CD 3, Track 13)

音声を聞いて空欄を適切な単語で埋めてください。

1. What are your _____?

Hello! How Are You?     Big or Small? Short or Tall?     Everyday Life

This Is My Family          Welcome to My Home

2. I like _____ and _____.

3. I like _____ horseback riding.

4. We _____ to go hiking in the mountains.

5. We also like to _____.

6. Bill loves _____.

7. Sue likes to _____.

8. Greg loves to _____ guitar, but Diane _____ to play piano.

9. Nicole _____ sewing.

10. Do you like _____ stamps or coins?

11. My parents like to _____ long _____.

12. Eddie likes _____.

13. We enjoy _____ during the summer.

答え

1. hobbies; 2. cooking, reading; 3. to go; 4. love; 5. go camping; 6. to bike; 7. go running; 8. play, prefers; 9. enjoys; 10. collecting; 11. take, walks; 12. to draw; 13. boating

# Grammar Builder 1

▶ 10C Grammar Builder 1 (CD 3, Track 14)

## LIKE を使って好きなことについて話す

like は英語でよく使われる動詞です。Like を使って人や物が好きであることを表現できます。

| I'm happy at my new job; I like my new boss a lot. | 私は新しい仕事場で幸せです。私の新しい上司が大好きです。 |

| I want to go to a Thai restaurant, because I like Thai food. | 私はタイ料理が好きなので、タイ料理の レストランに行きたいです。 |

like と一緒に to 不定詞形の動詞 (to go, to cook, to read) または –ing 形の動詞 (going, cooking, reading) を使うこともできます。

| I like to go to the library. I like going to the library. | 私は図書館に行くのが好きです。 |
| Pete likes cooking. Pete likes to cook. | ピートさんは料理をするのが好きです。 |
| We like to read. We like reading. | 私達は読書をするのが好きです。 |

a lot, really, very much といった表現を like と一緒に使うこともできます。

| My niece likes to go horseback riding a lot. | 私の姪は乗馬をするのがとても好きで す。 |
| John really likes collecting stamps. | ジョンさんは切手を集めるのがとても好 きです。 |
| My family likes to go boating very much. | 私の家族はボート漕ぎに行くのがとても 好きです。 |

否定文を作るには do/does not を使います。

| We don't like to sew. We don't like sewing. | 私達は裁縫をするのが好きではありま せん。 |
| She doesn't like to cook. She doesn't like cooking. | 彼女は料理をするのが好きではありま せん。 |

動詞の enjoy は like と似た意味を持っています。けれども後に続く動詞は –ing 形で なければいけません。

| Sarah enjoys reading the newspaper on Sunday mornings. | サラさんは日曜日の朝に新聞を読むの を楽しみます。 |

Hello! How Are You?    Big or Small? Short or Tall?    Everyday Life

This Is My Family    Welcome to My Home

| We enjoy having dinner with our friends. | 私達は友人と夕飯を食べるのを楽しみます。 |

Love は「大好きだ」という意味です。人や物が大好きである、愛している、と表現することもできますが、love to do や love doing という形を用いて「〜することが大好きだ」と表現することもできます。

| John loves his wife very much. | ジョンさんは奥さんをとても愛しています。 |
| Mary loves her children. | メアリーさんは彼女の子供達を愛しています。 |
| I love sushi! Let's go to a Japanese restaurant. | 私はおすしが大好きです！日本料理のレストランに行きましょう。 |
| We love relaxing and reading books on the weekends.<br>We love to relax and read books on the weekends. | 私達は週末にリラックスしたり本を読んだりするのが大好きです。 |

prefer は「より好きである」(like more) という意味です。

| I like watching television, but I prefer to read. | 私はテレビを見るのも好きですが、読書の方が好きです。 |
| We like camping, but we prefer going to the beach. | 私達はキャンプをするのも好きですが、ビーチに行く方が好きです。 |

何かが大嫌いであると表現したい場合は動詞 hate が使えます。hate の後に物や to 不定詞形の動詞や –ing 形の動詞を置きましょう。

| I hate sushi! I don't want to go to a Japanese restaurant. | 私はおすしが大嫌いです！日本料理のレストランには行きたくありません。 |
| The kids hate studying.<br>The kids hate to study. | 子供達は勉強するのが大嫌いです。 |

**Essential English**

doesn't like と似た意味を持つ表現には can't stand（耐えられない）もあります。人や物や動詞の –ing 形と一緒に使われます。

| Sheila can't stand her new boss. | シーラさんは新しい上司に耐えられません。 |
| Bob can't stand watching television. | ボブさんはテレビを見ることに耐えられません。 |

## Vocabulary Builder 2

▶ 10D Vocabulary Builder 2 (CD 3, Track 15)

| What do you feel like doing tonight? | あなたは今夜何がしたい気分ですか。 |
| I feel like seeing a movie. | 映画が見たい気分です。 |
| What's playing at the movies? | 何が上映されていますか。 |
| There's a romantic comedy, an action film, and a horror film. | ラブコメディーとアクションとホラー映画がやっています。 |
| I don't feel like seeing a horror film; let's see the romantic comedy. | ホラー映画を見る気分ではありません。ラブコメディーを見ましょう。 |
| We want to get together with friends at a restaurant. | 私達はレストランで友人と会いたいです。 |
| We're inviting friends to our place for a dinner party. | 私達は家に友人をディナーパーティーに招待します。 |
| John feels like seeing a play. | ジョンさんは劇を見たい気分です。 |
| Do you prefer the theater or the opera? | 演劇とオペラとどちらの方が好きですか。 |
| Bill can't stand the opera! | ビルさんはオペラには耐えられません！ |
| Josh wants to get together with friends this weekend to watch the football game. | ジョッシュさんは今週末に友人とフットボールの試合を見に行きたがっています。 |

Hello! How Are You?          Big or Small? Short or Tall?          Everyday Life

This Is My Family          Welcome to My Home

| I can't stand football; I prefer baseball. | 私はフットボールには耐えられません。野球の方が好きです。 |
| George doesn't play baseball, but he plays basketball. | ジョージさんは野球をしませんが、バスケットボールをします。 |
| I love soccer. It's a lot of fun! | 私はサッカーが大好きです。とても楽しいです！ |
| I can't stand soccer! It's boring. | 私はサッカーには耐えられません！つまらないです。 |
| No, it's not. Soccer is exciting! | いいえ、違います。サッカーはエキサイティングです！ |
| Let's play cards tonight. | 今夜トランプをしましょう。 |
| No, I feel like playing chess. | いいえ、私はチェスをしたい気分です。 |

## Take It Further

▶ 10E Take It Further (CD 3, Track 16)

feel like という表現が出てきましたね。want (to) と意味が似ています。

| What do you want to do tonight? What do you feel like doing tonight? | あなたは今夜何がしたいですか。 あなたは今夜何がしたい気分ですか。 |
| What do you feel like eating? I feel like pizza. | あなたは何を食べたい気分ですか。 ピザを食べたい気分です。 |

動詞 play は楽器を「演奏する」や、映画が「上映される」という意味で使うことができます。

| Greg loves to play guitar, but Diane prefers to play piano. | グレッグさんはギターを弾くのが大好きですが、ダイアンさんはピアノを弾く方が好きです。 |

**Essential English**

| What's playing at the movies? | 何が上映されていますか。 |
| A romantic comedy is playing. | |
| | ラブコメディーが上映されています。 |

play はスポーツを「する」という意味でも使われます。

| Paul loves to play basketball. | ポールさんはバスケットボールをするのが大好きです。 |
| John prefers to play football. | ジョンさんはフットボールをする方が好きです。 |
| Do you like playing tennis? | あなたはテニスをするのが好きですか。 |
| The high school students are playing football. | 高校生がフットボールをしています。 |
| Do you prefer to play football or soccer? | あなたはフットボールをするのとサッカーをするのとどちらの方が好きですか。 |

アメリカでは football は (American) football（アメフト）のことを指しますが、その他の多くの国では football というと、サッカー (soccer) のことを指します。

play は cards（トランプ）や chess（チェス）などのゲーム を「する」という意味でも使われます。

| Let's play cards tonight. | 今夜トランプをしましょう。 |
| No, I feel like playing chess. | いいえ、私はチェスがしたい気分です。 |

play は「遊ぶ」という意味としても使えます。

| The dog is playing with the cat. | 犬は猫と遊んでいます。 |
| The kids are playing outside. | 子供達は外で遊んでいます。 |

名詞の a play は「演劇」という意味です。

| Let's go to the theater and see a play. | 劇場に行って演劇を見ましょう。 |

Hello! How Are You?          Big or Small? Short or Tall?          Everyday Life

This Is My Family                    Welcome to My Home

# ✎ Vocabulary Practice 2

▶ 10F Vocabulary Practice 2 (CD 3, Track 17)

音声を聞いて空欄を適切な単語で埋めてください。

1. What do you _____ tonight?

2. I feel like _____ a movie.

3. What's _____ at the movies?

4. There's a romantic _____, an _____ film, and a
   _____ film.

5. I _____ seeing a horror film; let's see the
   romantic comedy.

6. We want to get _____ with friends at a restaurant.

7. We're _____ friends to our place for a dinner _____.

8. John feels like seeing a _____.

9. Do you prefer the _____ or the _____?

10. Bill _____ the opera!

11. Josh wants to _____ with friends this weekend to
    watch the football _____.

12. I can't stand _____; I prefer _____.

13. George doesn't _____ baseball, but he _____ basketball.

14. I _____ soccer. It's a lot of _____!

**Essential English**

Around Town | Let's Go Shopping | What Do You Feel Like Doing?

Let's Eat! | At Work

15. I can't stand soccer! It's _____!

16. No it's not. Soccer is _____!

17. Let's play _____ tonight.

18. No, I feel like playing _____.

**答え**

1. feel like doing; 2. seeing; 3. playing; 4. comedy, action, horror; 5. don't feel like; 6. together;
7. inviting, party; 8. play; 9. theater, opera; 10. can't stand; 11. get together, game; 12. football,
baseball; 13. play, plays; 14. love, fun; 15. boring; 16. exciting; 17. cards; 18. chess

# Grammar Builder 2

▶ 10G Grammar Builder 2 (CD 3, Track 18)

### 指示詞: THIS と THAT

**this** は自分の近くにある単数の物と一緒に使います。**these** は自分の近くにある複数の物と一緒に使います。

| This book is really interesting. | この本はとても面白いです。 |
| This book is really interesting. | この本はとても面白いです。 |
| These pants are very expensive. | このパンツはとても高いです。 |

**that** は自分の近くにはない単数の物と一緒に使います。**those** は自分の近くにはない複数の物と一緒に使います。

| That restaurant in the mall is not very good. | ショッピングモールのあのレストランはあまりよくありません。 |
| Those people in the park are playing soccer. | 公園にいるあの人達はサッカーをしています。 |

**this, that, these, those** の後には名詞 (book, pants, restaurant, people) を続けても続けなくても大丈夫です。

| Do you like that? | あれは好きですか? |
| No, I prefer this. | いいえ、これの方が好きです。 |

Hello! How Are You?          Big or Small? Short or Tall?          Everyday Life

This Is My Family                Welcome to My Home

| Are these your books? | これらはあなたの本ですか。 |
| Yes, those are my books. | はい、それらは私の本です。 |

this one や that one という表現方法もあります。

| That one is nice, but I prefer this one. | あれはいいですが、私はこれの方が好きです。 |
| I like this one, but that one is nicer. | 私はこれが好きですが、あれの方がいいですね。 |

## ✎ Work Out 1

▶ 10H Work Out 1 (CD 3, Track 19)

音声を聞いて空欄を埋めてください。

1. Do you like _____ chess?

2. No, I _____ playing chess. I _____ cards.

3. Do you _____ a romantic comedy?

4. No, I _____ romantic comedies! _____ see an action film.

5. They _____ to go camping.

6. I prefer to _____ home and _____.

7. Do you feel like _____ to a restaurant tonight?

8. Yes, let's go out. I _____ cooking.

9. Do you _____ collecting stamps?

10. No, collecting stamps is _____.

**答え**
1. playing; 2. can't stand, prefer; 3. feel like seeing; 4. hate, Let's; 5. really like; 6. stay, read; 7. going out; 8. don't feel like; 9. enjoy; 10. boring

**Essential English**

## 🎧 Bring It All Together

▶ 10I Bring It All Together (CD 3, Track 20)

ジェンさんとロブさんは週末の計画を立てています。聞いてみましょう。

| | |
|---|---|
| **Jen:** | **What do you feel like doing this weekend?** |
| ジェン： | 今週末は何をしたい気分？ |
| **Rob:** | **Nothing! I'm tired. I want to stay home and relax.** |
| ロブ： | 何もしたくないよ！疲れてるから家でリラックスしたい。 |
| **Jen:** | **Oh, come on. Let's do something. Ed and Sarah are having a dinner party on Saturday night.** |
| ジェン： | 何言ってるのよ。何かしましょうよ。エドとサラが土曜日にディナーパーティーを開くのよ。 |
| **Rob:** | **Ed and Sarah? You know I can't stand their food. They cook horrible food.** |
| ロブ： | エドとサラ？僕が彼らの出す食べ物に耐えられないのを知ってるだろ。料理がひどいよ。 |
| **Jen:** | **Come on. They're our friends, and they're inviting us to dinner. Just one night.** |
| ジェン： | 何言ってるの。友達なんだし、ディナーに誘ってくれたのよ。一晩だけだから。 |
| **Rob:** | **Well, I can have a big lunch and eat something before we go.** |
| ロブ： | うーん、昼ご飯をたくさん食べるか、出掛ける前に何か食べるかしておくことはできるな。 |
| **Jen:** | **Perfect. So, Saturday night we're visiting friends for dinner. What about Sunday?** |
| ジェン： | それでいいわ。じゃあ土曜の夜は友人宅でディナーね。日曜は？ |
| **Rob:** | **There's a football game on Sunday. I want to watch it.** |
| ロブ： | 日曜はフットボールの試合があるんだよ。それが見たいんだ。 |
| **Jen:** | **You want to spend your Sunday sitting in front of the television and watching a football game?** |

Hello! How Are You?      Big or Small? Short or Tall?      Everyday Life

This Is My Family      Welcome to My Home

| | |
|---|---|
| ジェン: | 日曜日をテレビの前に座ってフットボールの試合を見て過ごしたいっていうの？ |
| **Rob:** | **Yes.** |
| ロブ: | そう。 |
| **Jen:** | **That's boring!** |
| ジェン: | それはつまらないわ！ |
| **Rob:** | **No, football games are exciting!** |
| ロブ: | いや、フットボールの試合はエキサイティングだよ！ |
| **Jen:** | **Playing football is exciting, but sitting around watching television is boring.** |
| ジェン: | フットボールをするのはエキサイティングだけど、座ってテレビを見るのはつまらないわ。 |
| **Rob:** | **Well, what do you want to do?** |
| ロブ: | じゃあ君は何がしたいんだよ？ |
| **Jen:** | **The weather is nice. Let's go hiking.** |
| ジェン: | 天気がいいわ。ハイキングに行きましょうよ。 |
| **Rob:** | **Nah, I don't like hiking.** |
| ロブ: | いや、ハイキングは好きじゃないね。 |
| **Jen:** | **How about biking? We have new bikes.** |
| ジェン: | サイクリングはどう？新しい自転車があるでしょ。 |
| **Rob:** | **Yeah, that's true. And they're expensive. We should use them.** |
| ロブ: | まあそれはもっともだね。高かったし、使わなくちゃね。 |
| **Jen:** | **Perfect, so tomorrow we're having dinner with friends, and on Sunday we're going biking. A wonderful weekend.** |
| ジェン: | 完璧だわ。それじゃ、明日は友人とディナー。そして日曜日はサイクリングね。素晴らしい週末だわ。 |
| **Rob:** | **Okay, but Monday I'm staying in and watching television.** |
| ロブ: | オーケー。でも月曜日は家でテレビ見るからね。 |

**Essential English**

## ✎ Work Out 2

好き嫌いを言う練習をしましょう。括弧内の指示に従って、それぞれの質問に対する答えを書いてください。

例: **Do you like playing tennis? (Yes, very much.)**
答え: **Yes, I like playing tennis very much.**

1. **Do you like watching basketball games? (Yes.)**

   _____

2. **Does Bill like going camping? (No.)**

   _____

3. **Do you like horseback riding. (Yes, very much.)**

   _____

4. **Does Mary like cooking? (No, hates.)**

   _____

5. **Do the kids like doing homework? (No, can't stand.)**

   _____

6. **Does Jack like going to the movies? (Yes, loves.)**

   _____

7. **Does Marta like the opera? (Yes, but prefers the theater.)**

   _____

8. **Do you enjoy watching soccer on television? (Yes, but prefer playing.)**

   _____

Hello! How Are You?    Big or Small? Short or Tall?    Everyday Life

This Is My Family    Welcome to My Home

9. **Does Paul like to play chess? (No, not very much.)**

_____

10. **Does Sam like inviting friends over for dinner? (Yes, loves.)**

_____

**答え**
1. Yes, I like watching basketball games. 2. No, Bill doesn't like going camping. 3. Yes, I like horseback riding very much. 4. No, Mary hates cooking. 5. No, the kids can't stand doing homework. 6. Yes, Jack loves going to the movies. 7. Yes, Marta likes the opera, but she prefers the theater. 8. Yes, I enjoy watching soccer on television, but I prefer playing soccer. 9. No, Paul doesn't like to play chess very much. 10. Yes, Sam loves inviting friends over for dinner.

# ✎ Drive It Home

this, that, these, those の練習をしましょう。例に従って文を作ってください。

例: **The car is here. It is new.**
答え: **This car is new.**

1. **The book is here. It is boring.**

_____

2. **The food is here. It is very good.**

_____

3. **The horse is there. It is beautiful.**

_____

4. **The kids are there. They are playing on the computer.**

_____

5. **The people are here. They are watching a football game.**

_____

6. We are at the party. It is really boring.

_____

7. We are watching a movie. It is exciting.

_____

8. We do not have the bikes now. They are too expensive.

_____

答え:
1. This book is boring. 2. This food is very good. 3. That horse is beautiful. 4. Those kids are playing on the computer. 5. These people are watching a football game. 6. This party is really boring. 7. This movie is exciting. 8. Those bikes are too expensive.

## Parting Words

**Well done!** (よくできました!)これで *Essential English* の最後のレッスンが終了しました。学習した内容を確認してみましょう。

☐ 趣味に関する語彙　(まだ自信がない場合は p. 183 に戻って復習しましょう。)

☐ 好き (like) 嫌い (don't like) について話す　(まだ自信がない場合は p. 184 に戻って復習しましょう。)

☐ 余暇の過ごし方に関する語彙　(まだ自信がない場合は p. 187 に戻って復習しましょう。)

☐ 指示詞 this と that　(まだ自信がない場合は p. 191 に戻って復習しましょう。)

☐ 週末の計画についての会話の中で学習した項目を総合的に使う　(まだ自信がない場合は p. 193 に戻って復習しましょう。)

www.livinglanguage.com/languagelab のページをチェックするのを忘れずに。バーチャル単語帳やゲームやクイズで、学習したことを復習してみましょう!

# Word Recall

第10課で学習した重要語彙を復習しましょう。空欄を埋めてください。

A.

1. I enjoy _____ food and inviting my friends over for dinner.

2. Do you prefer _____ books or magazines?

3. I don't like _____ because I don't like horses.

4. We have a new bike, so tomorrow we're going _____.

B.

1. What are two musical instruments from this lesson?

   _____

2. What are two things from this lesson that some people enjoy collecting?

   _____

3. What do people enjoy doing on water, for example, in the ocean or on a lake?

   _____

4. What do people see at a theater?

   _____

5. Where do you go to see romantic comedies, action films, or horror films?

   _____

6. What kind of games do people enjoy watching on television?

   _____

7. If something isn't boring, it's …

   _____

8. What are two games that people play on a table?

   _____

# テスト2

## Quiz 2

第6課から第10課までで学習した内容を短いテスト形式で確認してみましょう。問題を解き終わったら自己採点をしてみてください。見直すべき箇所が見つかったら、まとめの会話に進む前に復習をしてください。
それでは復習テストを始めましょう。

A. どこで何を買いますか。

1. books, magazine, coffee          a. at an electronics store
2. computers, televisions, stereos  b. at a bakery
3. beef and pork                    c. at a hardware store
4. bread and cake                   d. at a convenience store
5. hammers and paint                e. at a butcher shop

B. some か any のどちらかで空欄を埋めてください。

1. We don't have _____ books in French.

2. I feel like drinking _____ tea.

3. Are there _____ good movies playing this weekend?

4. There aren't _____ nice pants in this store.

5. Please put _____ spinach on my plate.

C. much か many のどちらかで空欄を埋めてください。

1. How _____ children do you have?

2. I like horseback riding very _____.

3. There aren't _____ good stores at the mall.

4. I don't want too _____ sugar in my coffee.

5. You shouldn't drink so _____ cups of coffee.

D. 以下の各文を否定文、それから疑問文に直してください。

1. They're watching a football game.

   _____

2. Doctors work many hours at the hospital.

   _____

3. He gets to work by bus.

   _____

4. Her assistant eats lunch at twelve thirty.

   _____

5. They feel like cooking tonight.

   _____

E. 適切な動詞の形を選んでください。

1. I (work/am working) every weekday.

2. They (have/are having) a meeting right now.

3. We (go/are going) to the theater tomorrow night.

4. Bob (speaks/is speaking) four languages.

5. Architects (design/are designing) buildings.

**答え**

A. 1. d; 2. a; 3. e; 4. b; 5. c
B. 1. any; 2. some; 3. any; 4. any; 5. some
C. 1. many; 2. much; 3. many; 4. much; 5. many
D. 1. They aren't watching a football game. Are they watching a football game? 2. Doctors don't work many hours at the hospital. Do doctors work many hours at the hospital? 3. He doesn't get to work by bus. Does he get to work by bus? 4. Her assistant doesn't eat lunch at twelve thirty. Does her assistant eat lunch at twelve thirty? 5. They don't feel like cooking tonight. Do they feel like cooking tonight?
E. 1. work; 2. are having; 3. are going; 4. speaks; 5. design

# How Did You Do?

正解一つにつき一点として総合得点を出してみましょう。以下は得点に応じたアドバイスです。

**0-10 点:** もう一度レッスンに戻り、理解を確かめながら進めていくのがよいかもしれません。競争ではありませんから、急ぐ必要はないですよ!あわてずに各課のボキャブラリーや文法項目を注意深く見ていきましょう。

**11-18 点:** セクションAの問題を間違えた場合はボキャブラリーの項目に戻って復習するとよいでしょう。セクションB, C, D, Eの問題を間違えた場合は Grammar Builder に戻って文法の基礎をもう一度確認しましょう。

**19-25 点:** これまでの学習内容がしっかり頭に入っていますね!まとめの会話に進んでください!

点

# まとめの会話

5つの日常会話を通して、*Living Language Essential English* の全10課で学習した語彙や文法を練習してみましょう。それぞれの会話文の後には理解度を確認する質問が設けられています。発音の練習のために音声を聞くことも忘れないでください。

新しい単語や表現が出てくることもありますが、これはリアルで自然な日常会話が再現されているためです。分からない単語が出てきたら辞書を引いてくださいね。

## 🔊 Dialogue 1
▶ Dialogue 1A-1B (CD 3, Track 21-22)

新学期最初の授業で、サラさんはディエゴさんの隣に座ります。授業が始まる前に二人は自己紹介をして、ルームメートや家族のことについて話します。

| | |
|---|---|
| Sarah:<br>サラ: | Hi, I'm Sarah. What's your name?<br>こんにちは。私はサラ。あなたは? |
| Diego:<br>ディエゴ: | Oh hey. I'm Diego. Nice to meet you. Are you a freshman?<br>やあ。僕はディエゴ。はじめまして。君は一年生? |
| Sarah:<br>サラ: | Yes, I am.<br>そうよ。 |
| Diego:<br>ディエゴ: | Me too.<br>僕もだよ。 |
| Sarah:<br>サラ: | Where are you from?<br>どこから来たの? |
| Diego:<br>ディエゴ: | I'm from Puebla, Mexico.<br>メキシコのプエブラだよ。 |
| Sarah: | Oh, so you speak Spanish. I speak a little Spanish. I'm from Frankfurt, Germany. Do you speak German? |

| | |
|---|---|
| サラ: | あら、じゃあスペイン語を話すのね。私も少しスペイン語ができるわ。私はドイツのフランクフルト出身なの。あなたはドイツ語は話す？ |
| Diego: | **No, I only speak Spanish, English, and a little French. Do you live on campus?** |
| ディエゴ: | いや、僕はスペイン語と英語とフランス語を少しだけだね。君はキャンパスに住んでるの？ |
| Sarah: | **Yes, I live in a dorm room with two roommates, Yuko and Laura. Yuko is from Japan. I don't speak any Japanese, but she speaks English very well. Laura is from New York. Her English is pretty good!** |
| | [laughs] |
| サラ: | ええ、二人のルームメートと一緒に寮に住んでるの。裕子とローラよ。裕子は日本出身よ。私は日本語は全然できないけれど、彼女は英語がとても上手。ローラはニューヨーク出身で英語がなかなか上手だわ！ |
| | [笑] |
| Diego: | **I guess so! Is your dorm room big?** |
| ディエゴ: | だろうね！寮の部屋は広い？ |
| Sarah: | **No, it's quite small. And yours?** |
| サラ: | いいえ、かなり狭いわ。あなたの部屋は？ |
| Diego: | **I live in a house with my family. I have two brothers, David and Javier, and one sister, Anna. My brothers are 17 and 19, and my sister is 23. My parents are Luisa and Rogelio. My father is a professor and my mother is an engineer. Is your family big?** |
| ディエゴ: | 僕は家族と一緒に家に住んでるんだ。二人の男兄弟、デイビッドとハヴィアー、それから姉のアンナがいるんだ。デイビッドとハヴィアーは17歳と19歳で、姉は23歳。両親はルイーザとロヘリオ。父は教授で母はエンジニアなんだ。君のところは家族が多い？ |
| Sarah: | **Well, not really. I don't have any brothers and sisters, but I have lots of cousins. My father has four brothers and they all live near us.** |

| サラ: | うーん、そうでもないわ。私は兄弟がいないの。でもいとこがたくさんいるわ。父は4人兄弟がいて、みんな近くに住んでいるの。 |
|---|---|
| Diego: | So you live with just your parents? |
| ディエゴ: | じゃあ、家には君とご両親だけ? |
| Sarah: | No, I live with my grandmother and grandfather. My grandmother is 85 years old and my grandfather is 90! My grandmother is from France, so she also speaks French. |
| サラ: | いいえ、祖母と祖父がいるわ。祖母は85歳で祖父は90歳よ!祖母はフランス出身だからフランス語も話すわ。 |
| Diego: | Oh, here comes the professor. |
| ディエゴ: | あ、先生がいらしたよ。 |
| Sarah: | Let's talk more after class, okay? How about we go to the cafe near the dormitory? |
| サラ: | 授業の後でもっと話しましょ。寮の近くのカフェに行くのはどう? |
| Diego: | Sure! |
| ディエゴ: | うん、いいよ! |

# ✎ Dialogue 1 Practice

会話の内容が理解できたか確認するとともに、*Essential English*の第1課から第10課までで学習したことを復習しましょう。

A. 家族を表す適切な単語を空欄に埋めてください。

1. Your uncle's children are your _____.

2. Your mother's mother is your _____.

3. Your mother's father is your _____.

4. Your uncle's wife is your _____.

5. Your father's brother is your _____.

B. 以下の人物の出身国と国籍は何でしょうか。例に従って二つの文を書いてください。

例: (Diego) **Diego is from Mexico. He is Mexican.**

1. Sarah

   _____

2. Yuko

   _____

3. Laura

   _____

4. Sarah's grandmother

   _____

C. それぞれの質問に対し、会話の中に登場した人物の名前を書いて答えてください。

1. Who is 23? _____

2. Who speaks Japanese? _____

3. Who is an engineer? _____

4. Who is 90? _____

5. Who has four brothers? _____

**答え**
A. 1. cousins; 2. grandmother; 3. grandfather; 4. aunt; 5. uncle
B. 1. Sarah is from Germany. She is German. 2. Yuko is from Japan. She is Japanese. 3. Laura is from America. She is American. 4. Sarah's grandmother is from France. She is French.
C. 1. Diego's sister/Anna; 2. Yuko; 3. Diego's mother; 4. Sarah's grandfather; 5. Sarah's father

## 🎧 Dialogue 2

▶ Dialogue 2A-2B (CD 3, Track 23-24)

クリスティーナさんが両親の家についてビルさんに話しています。

| | |
|---|---|
| **Bill:** | Christina, do you live with your parents? |
| ビル: | クリスティーナ、君は両親と一緒に住んでるの? |
| **Christina:** | Yes, I do. Our house is far from the city center, but it's big and comfortable. |
| クリスティーナ: | ええ、そうよ。家は市の中心から離れているけど、大きくて心地いいわ。 |
| **Bill:** | How many bedrooms are there? |
| ビル: | 寝室はいくつあるの? |
| **Christina:** | There are three bedrooms, a living room, a dining room, and a kitchen. In the study, there are lots of books and a computer. I study in there because it is quiet. The kitchen is not big, but it's new. There is a stove, a refrigerator, and a long table. |
| クリスティーナ: | 寝室が三つに、リビング、ダイニング、それからキッチンがあるわ。それと書斎には本がたくさんとパソコンがあるの。静かだから私はそこで勉強してる。キッチンは広くないけど新しいわ。コンロと冷蔵庫と長テーブルがあるの。 |
| **Bill:** | Where is your bedroom? |
| ビル: | 君の寝室はどこ? |
| **Christina:** | It's between my parents' bedroom and the study. In my bedroom, there is a bed, a dresser, a bookshelf, and a desk. There are two windows, so it's very sunny. |
| クリスティーナ: | 両親の寝室と書斎の間よ。私の寝室にはベッドとたんすと本棚と机があるわ。窓が二つあるからとても日当たりがいいの。 |
| **Bill:** | Is there a bathroom next to your room? |
| ビル: | 君の部屋の隣にバスルームはある? |

| Christina: | No, but there is a bathroom next to my sister's room. There's a shower and a bathtub. The living room is under my parents' bedroom. There's a couch and a television. My dog sleeps on the couch. |
|---|---|
| クリスティーナ: | いいえ、でもバスルームは姉の部屋の隣にあるわ。バスルームにはシャワーとバスタブがあるの。リビングは両親の寝室のちょうど下ね。ソファーとテレビがあるわ。私の犬はソファーの上で寝るのよ。 |
| Bill: | Oh, you have a dog? Do you have a yard? |
| ビル: | ああ、犬がいるんだ。裏庭はある？ |
| Christina: | Yes. The yard is not big, but our dog is small, so it's okay. |
| クリスティーナ: | ええ。裏庭は大きくないけど、犬が小さいから大丈夫。 |
| Bill: | Do you have a picture of your family? |
| ビル: | 家族の写真はある？ |
| Christina: | Yes, here. These are my parents and this is my sister. |
| クリスティーナ: | ええ、これよ。これが両親でこれが姉。 |
| Bill: | Wow, she really looks like you. But she has long hair and yours is short. Is she a student? |
| ビル: | わあ、君ととてもよく似てるね。でもお姉さんは髪が長いけど、君は髪が短いね。お姉さんは学生？ |
| Christina: | No, she works for a company in New York City now. Her name is Ashley. She lives in an apartment there, but she comes home to my parents' house often. |
| クリスティーナ: | いいえ、姉は今ニューヨークの会社で働いているの。姉の名前はアシュリー。姉はニューヨークのアパートに住んでるけど、よく実家に帰ってくるわ。 |
| Bill: | That's nice. Okay, I have class now. See you tomorrow! |
| ビル: | それはいいね。えっと、もう授業だ。また明日ね！ |

Essential English

# ✎ Dialogue 2 Practice

A. 以下の形容詞の反意語を書いてください。答えとなる形容詞は会話の中に出てきています。

1. near _____

2. long _____

3. loud _____

4. old _____

B. 以下の文を yes/no で答えられる疑問文に変えてください。

例: The house is far.
答え: Is the house far?

1. The kitchen is sunny.

   _____

2. The house has three bedrooms.

   _____

3. Christina has a dog.

   _____

4. The dog is small.

   _____

5. Ashley and Christina are sisters.

   _____

C. どの部屋にどのアイテムがありますか。

1. stove
2. shower
3. dresser
4. computer
5. couch

a. bedroom
b. living room
c. kitchen
d. study
e. bathroom

### 答え

A. 1. far; 2. short; 3. quiet; 4. new
B. 1. Is the kitchen sunny? 2. Does the house have three bedrooms? 3. Does Christina have a dog? 4. Is the dog small? 5. Are Ashley and Christina sisters?
C. 1. c; 2. e; 3. a; 4. d 5. b

## ◖ Dialogue 3

▶ Dialogue 3A-3B (CD 3, Track 25-26)

サムさんは友人のジェニーさんの家に数日間泊まりに来ています。二人は、ジェニーさんの普段の生活や町について話しています。

| Jenny: | So, Sam, what do you want to do today? I don't have to go to work, so I can hang out all day. |
| ジェニー: | ねえ、サム、今日は何がしたい?会社に行かなくていいから一日中お供できるわよ。 |
| Sam: | Oh, great! Well, what do you usually do on weekends? |
| サム: | わあ、それは嬉しいね!えっと、普段週末は何をしてるの? |
| Jenny: | Hmm. Well, I get up late, usually around 10 a.m. Then, I shower and get dressed and go to the bakery on the corner. |
| ジェニー: | うーん。そうねえ、遅くまで寝てるわね。だいたい10時ぐらいまでかな。それからシャワーを浴びて、洋服を着て、すぐ角のパン屋に行くの。 |
| Sam: | What do you get at the bakery? |
| サム: | パン屋で何を買うの? |
| Jenny: | I get coffee and a pastry. Sometimes two. They're delicious! |
| ジェニー: | コーヒーと菓子パン一つよ。時々二つ。おいしいのよ! |

**Essential English**

| Sam: | And then what do you do? |
| サム: | それから何をするの？ |
| Jenny: | Well, on Saturday, there is a farmer's market at Hillside Park. |
| ジェニー: | えっと、土曜日はヒルサイド・パークでファーマーズマーケットがやってるわ。 |
| Sam: | Oh, where is that? Is it far? |
| サム: | えっ、それはどこ？遠い？ |
| Jenny: | No, it's not far. It's just a couple of miles away. |
| ジェニー: | いいえ、遠くないわよ。ここから2マイルぐらいね。 |
| Sam: | How do you get there? |
| サム: | どうやって行くの？ |
| Jenny: | I usually go by bus. The market is open until 3 p.m., but people buy all of the best produce by noon. |
| ジェニー: | 普通はバスで行くわ。マーケットは午後3時までやってるの。でも、いい物はみんなお昼までに売れちゃうわね。 |
| Sam: | Oh, I see. And then? What do you do next? |
| サム: | ああ、そうか。それから？普段マーケットの後は何するの？ |
| Jenny: | After I buy my groceries, I go home and put them away. By then, I'm hungry again! So, I make lunch. Then, I go to the gym with my friend, Emily. She lives across the street. We talk while we exercise. Do you exercise? |
| ジェニー: | 食べ物を買った後は、家に帰って買った物をしまうでしょ。その頃にはまたお腹が空いちゃうのよ！だからお昼を作るわ。それから友達のエミリーと一緒にジムへ行くの。エミリーは通りの向かいに住んでるわ。一緒に運動しながらおしゃべりするの。あなたは運動する？ |
| Sam: | I do sometimes. But when I'm on vacation, I don't exercise. It's a rule! |
| サム: | 時々ね。でも休みの時は運動しない。そういう風に決めてるんだ！ |
| Jenny: | I like that rule. Hey, I think there is a good movie showing right now. Do you want to see a movie? |
| ジェニー: | それはいい決まりだわ。ねえ、今いい映画がやってるみたいよ。映画見たい？ |

| Sam: | Sure. When does it start? |
|---|---|
| サム: | うん、もちろん。いつ始まる? |
| Jenny: | Hm, let's see. There are two showings: at half past one or two forty-five. |
| ジェニー: | えっと、二回上映があるわ。1時半と2時45分よ。 |
| Sam: | One thirty sounds good. But first, I want to try those pastries. Are you hungry? |
| サム: | 1時半がよさそうだね。でもまずはその菓子パンを食べてみたいな。君はお腹空いてる? |
| Jenny: | You know me! I'm always hungry! |
| ジェニー: | 私がいつもお腹空いてるのを知ってるでしょ! |

## ✎ Dialogue 3 Practice

A. 会話の内容に関する質問に答えてください。単語だけでなく、完全な文で答えてみましょう。

例: What does Jenny eat for breakfast?
答え: She eats pastries.

1. When does Jenny get up on her day off?

   _____

2. Where does Jenny buy coffee?

   _____

3. How does Jenny go to the farmers' market?

   _____

4. Who goes to the gym with Jenny?

   _____

**Essential English**

B. それぞれの時間を示す英語表現を選んでください。

1. 10:15                 a. **half past eight**

2. 8:30                 b. **twelve fifteen**

3. 2:45                 c. **noon**

4. 12:15                 d. **quarter past ten**

5. 12:00                 e. **two forty-five**

### 答え
A. 1. She gets up around 10:00 a.m. 2. She buys coffee at the bakery. 3. Jenny goes to the farmers' market by bus. 4. Jenny goes to the gym with her friend, Emily.
B. 1. d; 2. a; 3. e; 4. b; 5. c

## Dialogue 4
Dialogue 4A-4B (CD 3, Track 27-28)

ケイティーさんは結婚式に着ていくドレスを買わなければなりません。ボーイフレンドのマークさんと一緒にデパートへ買い物に出掛けようとしますが、マークさんは買い物が嫌いです。

| | |
|---|---|
| Mark: | **We're going to the department store? Do I have to come? Can I wait in the bookstore for you?** |
| マーク: | デパートに行くの?僕も行かなきゃだめ?本屋で待っててもいい? |
| Katie: | **No, you must come with me. I need your help! Besides, you are going to this wedding, too. You should buy a new jacket. Your old jacket is too small.** |
| ケイティー: | だめ、一緒に来てくれなきゃ。あなたの助けが必要なの!それにあなただって結婚式にいくのよ。新しいジャケットを買わなきゃだめじゃない。古いジャケットは小さすぎるでしょ。 |
| Mark: | **Who is getting married, again? I forget.** |
| マーク: | 誰が結婚するんだった?忘れちゃったよ。 |
| Katie: | **My cousin! She's a doctor, remember? She works at St. Francis Hospital.** |

| | |
|---|---|
| ケイティー: | 私のいとこよ!医者のいとこ。覚えてる?聖フランシス病院で働いてる。 |
| Mark: | **Oh, now I remember. Oh good. I can ask her about my foot problem.** |
| マーク: | ああ、思い出したよ。よし、僕の足の具合が悪いことを相談できるな。 |
| Katie: | **No, you can't! She is getting married. She doesn't need to talk about your feet that day! Now, which one is prettier, the blue dress or the silver dress?** |
| ケイティー: | だめよ!彼女は結婚するんだから、あなたの足のことなんて話してる場合じゃないわ!さてと、青いドレスとシルバーのドレス、どっちの方が綺麗? |
| Mark: | **How much do they cost?** |
| マーク: | 値段はいくら? |
| Katie: | **The blue dress is cheaper, but the silver dress is nicer. Don't you think?** |
| ケイティー: | 青いドレスの方が安いけど、シルバーのドレスの方がいいわ。そう思わない? |
| Mark: | **I like the blue one.** |
| マーク: | 僕は青いのが好きだな。 |
| Katie: | **Hm. Well, I think the silver one is better. I want to try it on. While I'm trying on the dress, you should look at the jackets. There are lots of different colors and styles.** |
| ケイティー: | うーん。私はシルバーの方がいいと思うけど。試着したいわ。ドレスを試着している間、ジャケットを見てきなさいよ。いろんな色やスタイルがあるわ。 |
| Mark: | **I want the most comfortable jacket. And I don't want to spend too much money.** |
| マーク: | 僕は一番着心地がいいジャケットが欲しいよ。それからあんまりお金をつぎこみたくない。 |
| Katie: | **You can find a jacket like that, I'm sure. And then, we have to buy some shoes and stockings. And a gift!** |

**Essential English**

| ケイティー: | そういうジャケットがきっと見つかるわよ。その後、靴とストッキングを買わなきゃ。それからプレゼントもね！ |
|---|---|
| Mark: | Hey, wait. Are you paying for this? I only have a little money. |
| マーク: | ちょっと待ってよ。支払いは君？僕はあんまりお金を持ってないよ。 |
| Katie: | It's fine. I'm paying for it. Now, go to the men's department and choose a jacket. The jacket should be warmer than your old jacket. It's winter. Oh and a belt! Then, we can meet at the cash register. |
| ケイティー: | 大丈夫。私が支払うわ。じゃあ、紳士服売り場へ行ってジャケットを選んでちょうだい。あなたの古いジャケットより暖かい物にした方がいいわ。冬なんだから。あ、それからベルトね！それからレジで会いましょ。 |
| Mark: | All right. Since you are paying for it, I guess I can't complain. |
| マーク: | わかったよ。君が支払うなら文句はないな。 |
| Katie: | Exactly. Now, go! |
| ケイティー: | その通り。はい、じゃあ行って！ |

## ✎ Dialogue 4 Practice

A. 会話の中で出てきた単語を空欄に埋めてください。

1. The blue dress is cheaper but the silver dress is _____.

2. No, you _____ come with me.

3. While I am trying on the dress, you _____ look at the jackets.

4. Now, go to the _____ and choose a

   jacket.

5. Since you are _____ for it, I guess I can't complain.

B. 以下の形容詞の比較級と最上級を書いてください。

1. big _____

2. warm _____

3. comfortable _____

4. cheap _____

5. pretty _____

**答え**
A. 1. nicer; 2. must; 3. should; 4. men's department; 5. paying
B. 1. bigger, biggest; 2. warmer, warmest; 3. more comfortable, most comfortable; 4. cheaper, cheapest; 5. prettier, prettiest

## 🗨 Dialogue 5
▶ Dialogue 5A-5B (CD 3, Track 29-30)

ショーンさんとキャラさんはブラインド・デート（初対面のデート）をしています。二人は仕事や趣味について話しています。

| | |
|---|---|
| Sean: | Is this table okay? |
| ショーン: | このテーブルでいいかな。 |
| Kara: | Hm, how about that table? It's quieter over there. |
| キャラ: | えっと、あっちのテーブルはどう？あっちの方が静かよ。 |
| Sean: | Sure! So, tell me about yourself. What do you do? |
| ショーン: | もちろん！えっと、君のことについて話してよ。仕事は何をしてるの？ |
| Kara: | Well, I'm an office manager. So, you know, I organize the office: schedule meetings, buy supplies, and direct phone calls and emails. I work from nine to five on weekdays. I like my job a lot. My boss is really nice. She's an architect. What about you? What do you do? |
| キャラ: | えっと、私はオフィスマネージャーをしてるわ。だから、事務の管理をしてるの。会議のスケジュールを入れたり、必要な物を購入して揃えたり、電話やメールを受けたり。平日の9時から5時まで仕事するわ。自分の仕事が大好きよ。上司はとてもいい人で、建築家なの。あなたは？何をしてるの？ |

Essential English

| | |
|---|---|
| Sean: | I'm a cook at a restaurant. I love making new dishes, so it's very exciting. But I don't like the schedule. I work from four o'clock until midnight. And I have to work on weekends. |
| ショーン: | 僕はレストランで調理師をしているんだ。新しい料理を作るのが大好きだから、とてもエキサイティングだよ。でもスケジュールに関しては不満があるね。4時から夜の12時まで働くんだ。それから週末も仕事だよ。 |
| Kara: | Oh, that's too bad. But shouldn't you be at work right now? It's seven o'clock. |
| キャラ: | まぁ、それは大変ね。今仕事しなきゃいけない時間なんじゃないの？7時よ。 |
| Sean: | No, I don't work on Mondays. It's my night off. And here I am, in a restaurant! |
| ショーン: | いや、月曜は働かないんだ。休みの夜だね。でも今僕はレストランにいるし！ |
| Kara: | Yeah, I guess you can't escape it! Well, tonight you don't have to cook at least. |
| キャラ: | そうね、レストランからは逃れられないみたいね！まあ少なくとも今夜は料理しなくていいけどね。 |
| Sean: | That's true. What do you usually do on weekends? Do you have any hobbies? |
| ショーン: | そうだね。君は週末はたいてい何をするの？何か趣味はある？ |
| Kara: | I love to play soccer, so I often go to the park and play a game with my friends. Do you play soccer? |
| キャラ: | 私はサッカーをするのが大好きよ。だから公園によく行って、友達と試合をするの。あなたはサッカーはする？ |
| Sean: | No, but I love watching it. Do you have any other hobbies? |
| ショーン: | いや、でも見るのは大好きだよ。他には趣味はある？ |
| Kara: | I like going to the movies a lot. |
| キャラ: | 映画に行くのが大好きね。 |
| Sean: | Me too! Do you feel like seeing a movie this weekend? I finish work early, around six o'clock. |

| | |
|---|---|
| ショーン: | 僕もだよ！今週末映画に行かない？仕事が早く終わるから。6時ぐらいに。 |
| Kara: | **That sounds great! What do you prefer: horror movies, romantic comedies, science fiction … ?** |
| キャラ: | それはいいわ！ホラーとラブコメディとSFと、どれがいい？ |
| Sean: | **I don't like romantic comedies or science fiction, but I love watching horror movies.** |
| ショーン: | ラブコメディーやSFは好きじゃないな。でもホラーは大好きだよ。 |
| Kara: | **Me too! Perfect. The Claw is playing this weekend, I think. Do you want to see that?** |
| キャラ: | 私も！完璧ね。「クロー」が今週末やってると思う。見たい？ |
| Sean: | **Yeah! Oh, here comes the waiter. We should look at the menu. Do you know what you want?** |
| ショーン: | うん！あ、ウェイターが来るよ。メニュー見なきゃね。何を頼みたい？ |
| Kara: | **I want a cheeseburger, with French fries.** |
| キャラ: | 私はチーズバーガーとポテトがいいわ。 |
| Sean: | **Me too! What a coincidence. I feel like we have a lot in common. Don't you?** |
| ショーン: | 僕も！偶然だなあ。僕達って共通点が多いと思わない？ |
| Kara: | **Yes, I do, too.** |
| キャラ: | ええ、私もそう思うわ。 |

# ✎ Dialogue 5 Practice

A. 括弧内の表現を使って現在進行形の文を作成してください。

例: **It's Sunday afternoon. Sean (to watch a soccer game)**
答え: **Sean is watching a soccer game.**

1. **It's 7:30 p.m. Sean (to work)**

**Essential English**

2. It's 5 p.m. on Monday. Kara (to leave her office)

   _____

3. It's Monday night. Sean and Kara (to have dinner)

   _____

4. It's Saturday night. Sean and Kara (to watch a horror movie)

   _____

5. It's Sunday afternoon. Kara and her friends (to play soccer)

   _____

B. それぞれの文を続けるのに適切な表現を選んでください。

1. Kara is ...

   a. a teacher.

   b. an engineer.

   c. an architect.

   d. an office manager.

2. Sean doesn't like ...

   a. to watch soccer.

   b. to watch horror movies.

   c. his schedule.

   d. cheeseburgers.

3. Sean ...

   a. works on Mondays.

b. hates his job.

c. loves science fiction.

d. likes making new dishes.

**答え**

A. 1. Sean is working. 2. Kara is leaving her office. 3. Sean and Kara are having dinner. 4. Sean and Kara are watching a horror movie. 5. Kara and her friends are playing soccer.

B. 1. d; 2. c; 3. d